Brain Hacking:

Rewire Your Mind to Have

It All

By Adam Lyons

Brain Hacking: Rewire Your Mind to Have It All

ISBN-13: 978-1987526998

ISBN-10: 1987526996

Cover design by Sooraj Mathew

Table of Contents

Introduction

In this book, I'm going to challenge the way you think. Literally. My goal is to get you to start listening to those little voices in your head, and to not only hear them but to understand them. You may find it hard to accept but bear with me, and I promise you will see that some of those voices have an agenda, and once you learn to identify which of the voices have your best interests in mind, you can take those first few crucial steps to have the most amazing life possible.

This book contains the technique I used to transform my life from being a poor kid growing up in a housing project in East London with no hope of ever getting a girlfriend...to being a successful man who lives on a 40-acre estate in Texas with my four children, five cats, and two girlfriends.

You can find the same success. And it all starts with doing one thing.

Chapter 1: Why You Should Kill the Negative Voice in Your Head—Now!

When we're children, we have dreams, things we *know* we're going to do as we get older. I was going to be a robot engineer. I was so sure of it. But over time things change. The dreams of our childhood disappear as more practical events start to demand our attention. It starts so simply—we put off a task here to earn money there, we skip a trip today to have money for a deposit on a loan later.

Before you know it, we've developed an amazing ability to tell ourselves *no*.

Sadly, that thought pattern turns into a powerful force in our head. It becomes a negative voice that tells us that we can't do something. Eventually, it becomes so pervasive it can feel like it's the only voice in our head at times, telling us that we don't deserve that job promotion, we can't get to the gym, we don't deserve to date someone better.

Sometimes that voice becomes so powerful we let it make decisions for us. We let it stop us from doing the things we know we need to do to live the life we want to live.

It doesn't have to be that way.

If we want to earn more money...

If we want the perfect relationship...

If we want to be proud of how we look...

If we want to be more successful...
...we have to hack our brains.

We do this by removing the negative voice that sits inside our brain and getting it to shut up and listen for a change.

My name is Adam Lyons, and in this book, I'm going to teach you how to do exactly that.

I'm going to teach you how to destroy the negative voice in your head with one incredibly easy step.

Now, I'm pretty sure you already know exactly what I'm talking about when I say that "negative voice in your head." What's so funny about it is that for many people, that negative voice plays such an active role in their life. It's constantly telling them things they cannot do.

It's like, "You can't date someone you want because they wouldn't be into you." Or, "You can't get that job promotion you want because you're not good enough." Or, "You could never run a marathon; that's far...too far." Or, "You want to work out? Oh no, that's just for people who do lots of steroids and put loads of time into it. You can't do that."

We all have that voice that always tells us we're not good enough for something.

"You're not going to pass that exam."

"That person is going to make fun of you."

"That person thinks you're ugly."

"You can't do it..."

"You will fail..."

"It's a waste of time..."

That horrible voice holds all of us back, and the shocking thing about it is we never hear anybody else's.

Did you ever think about that? It is your negative voice. It lives inside your head, and it sits and feeds on you and your sadness, and its purpose is purely to stop you from doing things that could make you successful.

In this book, I'm going to explain to you why it exists and what its real purpose is, and more importantly, I'm going to tell you how you can destroy it forever. Yes, you can literally kill that negative voice. I did it myself, and my life has completely turned around, and it is going to do exactly the same for you.

There are successful people all over the world that you can look at and instantly know that they've killed their negative voice. It's gone, and now they don't have it. Look at people like Warren Buffett and Tony Robbins. I know they have killed that voice. Or if they haven't killed it, then they have severely hampered its ability to hold them back.

The funny thing is, the only thing stopping you from being the next Warren Buffett, from being the next Tony Robbins, heck from just being the most successful person that you know, is that negative voice.

In this book, we're going to start by breaking down the psychology behind the negative voice. We're going to talk about how the brain works and why that voice even exists, what its natural purpose is, and why it is okay to destroy it.

In many ways, the negative voice is almost like your appendix. It used to have a purpose, but it's not needed anymore, and keeping hold of it can only cause you problems.

Take a moment and imagine having all the money you could want, all the things that you've ever wanted, and being able to do all the things you've ever wanted to do.

Now, imagine the only reason you don't have them is because that little voice in your head tells you that you can't get that promotion, you can't set up your own business, or you can't do whatever it is you want to do.

How bad would you want that negative voice gone?

You've probably heard other people expressing theirs from time to time: Imagine having a great body and when you walk into a room, everyone says, "Oh, my God, your body looks amazing. How did you do that? Every time I try and work out, I get tired, I can't lift enough weights, or I get sick."

Whatever the excuse you hear at the end of their comment, you know it was their negative voice.

If you can lose that negative voice:

- You're going to be able to get in shape.
- You're going to earn more money.

- You're going to have the relationship you want. You're going to be able to do all these wonderful things.

I want to start by sharing one of my own stories with you. This is one way my negative voice hurt me. I'm going to tell you how my negative voice was keeping me in a very damaging relationship. It not only almost crippled my entire life financially and romantically, it almost completely destroyed my self-esteem.

By killing that negative voice, I managed to get out of that relationship and completely turn my life around. I went from a terrible relationship to being voted the number one dating coach in the world, three years in a row, and being recognized on multiple media outlets. I was interviewed for documentaries, and you may have seen the articles and news reports around the world talking not only about my own dating life with my two girlfriends but how I helped to improve other people's dating life easily.

The only reason that happened, the only reason I am who I am today, is because I learned how to turn off that negative voice in my head.

I want you to make yourself a promise.

I used to have that negative voice in my head before I killed it, so I'm going to assume that you've got one, too. If you can admit that you have that negative voice, if what I'm saying makes sense to you, then make yourself a promise.

Get a pen, get out your phone, whatever you want to use to do this exercise. But write down one little phrase.

"I'm going to kill that negative voice in my head."

Can you promise you will do that?

Now, I'm going to make another assumption: Despite liking the idea of writing down that phrase, I'm going to assume you didn't do it.

The reason is that negative voice.

It probably said something like "I don't actually need to write it" or "imagining doing it is as good as doing it" or "I'll do it later." Whatever the excuse is, you didn't do it. So now you have another chance.

Write it down.

This is the funny thing about success. People always complain they don't have what they want, but they struggle to take the steps they need to take to get the results they want.

Often the tasks are as simple as writing something down. Yet people listen to that negative voice and don't take action, and the next thing you know you've developed a habit of *not* doing the things you should be doing to improve your life.

If you can manage to write that phrase down, you're a lot closer to killing that negative voice than you would believe.

I'm not the only one who has managed to kill this negative voice. As I said, there are a whole bunch of successful people who've managed to kill it. Again, there's Warren Buffett, the big financial investor. He's a multi-billionaire. He's got ridiculous amounts of money. There's Neil Strauss, a good friend of mine and one of the most successful dating experts in the world. Both of these people applied one very simple technique to get rid of that negative voice and become successful.

I know it sounds crazy right now, but I'm going to tell you what they did. I'm going to tell you what I did. If you think of any successful person, well, I guarantee that by the end of this book, you're going to be able to type that person's name into a search engine and you are going to see that the evidence of what I'm talking about is real.

Remember to Google it. Make that promise to yourself; trust me, you will need the positive reinforcement, so the voice of negativity will stay dead. It's important to see actual proof that the people in the world who are successful have all done what I'm about to share with you.

Here's where you are going to be even better than them, however, because you're going to know the psychology behind why it works and how a very special psychologist by the name of Sigmund Freud was one of the first people to identify this voice.

Some of the discoveries I've made over the last few years really build upon his work. As you'll see, what I've learned will not only help you to identify that voice, it's the key to destroying it.

Next Steps: If you want to hear more about my discoveries, and how much they've helped both the people I've worked with over the years and me, I'd heavily recommend checking out the Facebook page for one of my companies, Psychology Hacker. I'll tell you more about them later, but I built it from the ground-up to help good people kill that negative voice.

Take the steps to kill that voice and use this link to access **three simple techniques** that will have you thinking positive: PsychologyHacker.com/Positive

Chapter 2: Understanding Why There Is a Negative Voice in Your Head

Right now, you probably think the voice in your head is yours. Well, I've got some news for you. It isn't. It's not actually your voice.

This negative voice in your head was identified by Sigmund Freud over a hundred years ago now. He identified three distinct voices in our head, and each one has a different purpose and way of communicating with us.

Now, I'm not going to teach you Sigmund Freud's works. Mostly because I don't agree with everything he teaches, but also because I don't want to bore you with complicated psychological theory.

Instead, I'm going to share with you something that I have observed and studied myself over the past 10 years of helping people achieve success and working with some of the world's leading psychologists.

I like to think of it as a little bit more practical, and a little bit easier to use.

Those three voices in your mind function very differently, even if they sound exactly the same.

If you speak a different language, you may have noticed that the voice in your head can change languages. In fact, it's very difficult for people to speak a different language without the voice in their head changing to speak that same language.

This should show you that the voice in your head isn't static. It changes. It can change the language it speaks. It can change its attitude. It can change its mood.

It's not actually just the one voice changing either. It's not your voice changing. It isn't *you* changing.

It is the three voices of your subconscious talking and arguing amongst themselves. Believe it or not, none of those voices are actually you.

You may remember those old cartoons where the character has an angel on one shoulder and a devil on the other. The angel is trying to tell the character to do good things while the devil is trying to tell him or her to do bad things. The character in the middle, of course, is trapped in between trying to decide what to do.

Our experiences with our voices are almost exactly like that, except there are three voices instead of two.

Also, they don't try and convince *you* what to do. They fight amongst each other, and then once *they* decide what to do, they often make the decision for you.

They have a huge battle between them, and the winner gets to tell you what to do. If you aren't careful, they will make you do things or, more often than not...*not* do things.

Those three voices can basically mind-control you into doing whatever they want you to do.

And what's scarier still is most people just let their voices control them.

Each of the three voices is completely different. So, let's take a moment to meet those three voices inside your head and discuss their function and what they do.

The first voice I like to refer to as your "true fan." Now, the true fan loves you. The true fan thinks that you deserve everything. It's the little voice telling you that "you *can* do it!"

If you're not sure what the true fan sounds like, if your little voice of positivity isn't raising its head all the time, then you can be sure that your negative voice, the negative part of your brain, is dominating.

That means you really need to read through to the very end of this book because a large part of it is learning how to wake up your true fan.

The true fan is wonderful. When the true fan kicks in, you feel great because it tells you how great you are all the time. The true fan is like:

"You can do this!"

"You can make it happen!"

"You should do that!"

It's constantly telling you all these great, wonderful things that you can do and that you should do. In a perfect world, we want the true fan to be the biggest, strongest, most powerful voice in our head.

When your true fan is the loudest voice in your head, it will help you find solutions to life's problems.

If you're thinking, *hmm, I'm really not sure what I should do about this conundrum at work*, or *I don't know how to handle this problem in my dating life*, the true fan will say to you, *you know what worked before, you should try this.*

Then you will think, *thanks, brain. That's so useful. I'm going to do that.*

That's what the true fan does. It helps you get things done. The problem is that the true fan is in a constant state of war with the negative voice, which can be incredibly powerful. In fact, for most people, thanks to the pressures and expectations of modern society, it's the dominant one of the two. So, when the true fan and the negative voice go to war, for most people the negative voice usually wins.

Watch a video of Tony Robbins, Warren Buffett or any other super-successful person, and you will see that they do not have that negative voice holding them back. Their true fan is the winner in every single conflict in their head. Warren Buffett never thinks *you know what? I shouldn't invest any money in anything right now because everything is horrible, so I'm really, really scared and I'm never going to invest again.* No, he makes careful decisions. He's not going to invest in something that doesn't make sense, but Warren Buffett will invest where he knows it makes sense because the true fan in him says, *hey, that's the thing to do.* The negative voice doesn't hold him back. He listens to the true fan. He invests when he needs to.

It's the same with Tony Robbins. When Tony Robbins stands on stage and motivates people, he's not thinking, *man, maybe I can't do it today. Maybe no one is going to do what I want.*

No, Tony Robbins thinks, *I'm going to do this.*

At the beginning of Tony Robbins' career, he actually contacted the American military and said that he could improve their ability to shoot pistols. He did this even though he had no experience of doing it in the past, and he succeeded! It was because he believed that he was capable of doing it.

It's not just belief alone, and it didn't come out of nowhere. It was his true fan telling him he could do it.

I did mention there are three voices and it's true. There's a third voice involved in this war, and that third voice is the mentor.

The mentor is literally the sum of all your past experiences. It's the voice of your parents, your teachers, the stories you've heard, the books you've read, and all your life experiences.

The mentor remembers what you have learned in the past, and it brings up that "evidence" to help the other two voices make a decision.

It's the mentor's job to stop a stalemate.

If you can visualize the fight between the voices if you've got the true fan on one side and the negative voice on the other, the mentor is the ally. It can move and help either one.

Whoever gets the mentor wins the fight, as it's two against one.

If the negative voice gains the mentor, then it's two against one against the true fan and the true fan shuts down. The true fan suddenly can't communicate, can't win. It's beaten up by the other two. That frees the negative voice to tell you; *you can't succeed. You can't get anywhere. You can't make this happen.* So, you make the decision that you shouldn't go for it.

Take a moment and reflect on this.

Write down just one thing that the negative voice has stopped you gaining in life recently, whether it was going for a new work opportunity, talking to someone you were attracted to, or maybe working out. Maybe you felt you could do it, but you didn't really feel up to it.

Write one sentence or one word of what you didn't do, that's what the negative voice stopped you from achieving.

Realize that the only reason it has been capable of stopping you from getting what you wanted was that it allied with your mentor and it shut down your true fan.

Because your true fan wasn't able to fight back, you didn't get what was written on that note.

During the fight, the true fan was screaming, "Hey, you should totally go for it!" Meanwhile, the negative voice said, "It's never going to happen. You're never going to succeed. You're going to fail. You're going to look stupid. People are going to laugh at you."

Your negative voice looked to the mentor and said, "Mentor, do you agree with me?"

The mentor in that particular situation said, "Yeah, you're going to fail. Experience has proven it. The last seven times you tried to do it, you failed, and you didn't get anywhere and so don't bother. You're just going to get disappointed. It's just not going to work. You're not going to be able to lift the weights. You're going to look silly in front of everybody, and you're going to fail."

This is why people get stuck in bad situations. They want out. But their internal monologue is against them. It's two versus one in almost every decision to improve their life.

What's worse, the more your voices say no, the more "evidence" the mentor has that the negative voice is correct. The more you listen to the negative voice, the more the mentor believes that you actually *want* to follow the decision not to change things.

Sadly, because of this, it's easy to get stuck living in a situation that makes you miserable. I was living with my girlfriend, and it was terrible. I shouldn't have been there, and yet I was. I didn't feel like I could get out of the situation because my negative voice was holding me back, and my mentor was confirming that I wanted to stay there!

This internal mental war goes on and on every day, and for you to win it, you need the mentor to shift sides. Because when your mentor allies with your true fan, the negative voice can't win. It literally cannot. It can't beat both voices.

So, the moment your mentor is on the wrong side, it's aiding the negative voice. All the experience of all the bad things that have happened to you in your past are weighing up, and the negative voice says, "Look at all this evidence." The mentor chimes in with, "Yeah, look at this evidence of all this failure you've had. You can't do it." The positive voice, your true fan, is like, "I think you can do it," but it's not enough.

Your consciousness after seeing the war between the three of them gives up. The negative voice and the mentor win.

One of the discoveries I've made is that it is possible for you to override those voices completely. They're not you. They're just thought processes. In the same way that you can change what language they speak, or what you want to think about, or what direction you want to walk in, you can *force* any decision you want.

The way you do this is by using your brain actively.

This is something that blows people's minds. Our brain has two functions: You've got active mode, and you've got passive mode. The sad fact is that most people go through life just living in their passive mode.

You can think of the passive mode as running around with your subconscious making decisions about your life. When you're in passive mode, you're choosing not to engage your thought patterns, and instead, you're relying on your three inner voices to make the decisions. It's almost like having three advisors, and the king just never makes a decision.

If you've ever watched the TV show *Game of Thrones*, you can imagine a king thinking, *I don't really know what to do, so I'm just not going to make a decision. I'm going to go and hang out and have sex with people every so often and spend money and go hunting.*"

The three advisors are running everything. The one good advisor, the true fan, is saying things like, "Hey, we should probably do something to help the kingdom."

The negative voice says, "No, that's just going to fail. We shouldn't do it."

The mentor has all these experiences from the king's past bad decisions and is aiding the negative voice, saying, "Yeah, everything is going to fail if we do anything so let's let everything fall apart."

The whole kingdom falls apart, and everyone dies. (Which is actually a pretty common occurrence in that show.)

There is, however, an alternative.

Instead, you can actively engage your brain, and you can choose to be an active king. You can take control of your life and say, "I'm going to decide where I want to go and what I'm going to do."

I run a consultancy where I help people grow their business, and I use these concepts to improve every area of their lives. After completing my training, one of my students developed an international sales company earning up to $60,000 a week. He was a big fan of the way that I think and solve problems, and he had a great way of summarizing everything with analogies to confirm he understood my training.

He had this great analogy to explain this concept, which is if you were on a ship, and it was your own ship, what position do you think you would take?

Once again, pause and do the exercise. What position would you take if you were on a ship and you could have any role?

Almost everybody says, "It's my ship, I'd be the captain."

Well, guess what? Your body is your ship, and if you're not actively engaging your brain, not actively doing the things you want to do or know you should be doing...you're not the captain.

Instead, you're allowing your three subordinates to control the ship. If you have ever felt the negative voice holding you back from doing something you wanted, from attempting to succeed at something, you're not the captain of your ship. If you *were* the captain, you would be telling it where to go, and it would do what you want. Most people live in the passive mode of their brain, so they don't actively control their ship.

When you let the three voices make decisions for you, you're trusting somebody else to steer your course. You're letting that negative voice control the ship, and it does what it wants. And what it does …is nothing. It makes you not do a single damn thing.

I was proud of my student for this realization he had. He'd go off and teach people about it. I loved it so much that I wanted to share it here with you, because I think you probably realize that on the one hand, you feel that negative voice holding you back, yet, on the other hand, you're like, "If I had a ship, I'd be the captain."

Your body is your ship, and if you're not doing what you want in life, you're not in charge of it.

Next steps: If you want to start steering your ship, there is no better time in the world to do it than today. As I mentioned earlier, so much of the impact of the mentor is driven by past experience; the most positive experiences you have, the better. That's why I release a video every day on Facebook, where I just talk about my life and my experiences. You'll hear a lot of it in the upcoming chapters, but if you're looking for evidence that you can do anything in life that you want to, those videos are a great place to start. Try out the link below to see one particular story that I think really encapsulates this mindset: PsychologyHacker.com/HoldingBack

Chapter 3: An Experiment to Introduce You to Your Subconscious

By now you should realize you need to take control. You've got to say, "You know what? I want to control my own ship. I want to take it by the wheel and take it where I want it to go."

(As I write this I realize I have no idea if ships have a wheel. But I'm pretty sure I've seen old pirate ships with wheels, so we'll assume your ship has a wheel.)

You're going to take it, and you're going to steer it. You want to go and get all the success you want, whether it's financial, whether it's your health, whether it's your perfect dating life. Whatever it is that you want, you have to grab that wheel, and you have to steer it.

In this chapter, I'm going to show you how most people are in passive mode. I'm going to show you an experiment so you can see how easy it is to coast through life in passive mode. And then I'm going to introduce you to your subconscious so you can see what it looks like when it takes control.

For this experiment, you're going to answer two questions. You'll need to write your answers down somewhere. (Thankfully you can just put them next to the previous things you wrote...right? Unless of course that negative voice still had control of you. If so, it's time to start beating it back and taking control.)

For the first question, it's very important you don't cheat and Google the answer.

What percentage of marriages end in divorce?

Write down your answer.

The next question is very straightforward: I want you to attempt to solve this mathematical equation. $76,328 \times 3,561 = $ _____

Just write your answer down somewhere.

Now assuming you actually did the tasks, your answers should be very revealing.

The answers themselves are not as important as the thought processes that went into them.

When I asked the first question, even if you didn't write down the answer, you probably felt the answer was somewhere around 40 to 60 percent.

However, you probably didn't even attempt to answer the second question.

I'm not psychic. It's simply understanding how the voices in your head work. The funny thing is, of the two questions, only one of them was easily solvable. The second one.

Your inner voices give an easy answer to the first question because they make it up. You don't actually know the percentage of marriages that end in divorce. You think you do. You may even "remember" hearing the figure somewhere, but you're unlikely to know where.

These are your inner voices making decisions for you. The true fan suggested you could answer, and the mentor gave some random figure that vaguely sounded right.

Your negative voice never turned up because there was zero fear of me correcting you. After all, I'm just an author of a book.

The second question is more telling, however. When given a mathematical equation that was solvable, unless you've already started to get a grip on that negative voice, you're unlikely to have bothered solving the equation.

The answer is 271,804,008 in case you are curious.

It's a simple answer, which I found by using the calculator on my phone. I never said you couldn't use a calculator to solve it, but the reality is you probably didn't even bother attempting to answer—you decided it was too difficult.

Or should I say your negative voice told you it was? It decided it wasn't worth answering, convincing you that you could "get through the book" without answering it.

And that's how the negative voice holds you back.

We all did math problems at school. You could have solved that equation, but you didn't. This theory comes from a book by Daniel Kahneman called *Thinking, Fast and Slow*.

I like to think of it as active control versus passive control of your brain. What happens is most of us go through life using our passive brain. This is simply because your brain wants to keep you alive. This is why that negative voice has so much control over you.

You see, to engage the active part of your brain, the thinking part, the part that could have solved the sum in the second question, you needed to engage the cerebral cortex, which is the part of your brain that can solve problems. However, that part of your brain takes more energy to use than any other part of your brain because it's the newest part.

Humans haven't really been around on Earth for a very long time. In fact, if you condensed the entirety of life on the planet down to a single day, human beings don't turn up until around 11:59 p.m. It's crazy. We're at the very end of the day in the earth's hypothetical 24-hour life because we are simply that new to the planet.

So, we haven't been around for a long time, and the cerebral cortex part of our brain is the newest part. It's the freshest part. Because it's new, it's got all these teething issues. The biggest teething issue is it takes energy.

It's like when the latest iPhone or Android phone hits the market. When the newest one comes out, it comes with a new operating system. That operating system is then updated on all the older phones, and because the older hardware isn't used to the new software, it sucks the life out of the battery.

The more times they update the new software, the more the battery life in the older phones gets worse and worse and worse because it can't cope with all the awesome new processes.

Your brain is exactly the same.

Over the last 100 years, our operating system has drastically improved, from using phones to the internet, to virtual reality and more. Yet our hardware is the same hardware that the Stone Age humans had.

In short, thinking takes energy. *Lots* of it.

For you to be active, you need to have that active part of your brain engaged and working, and this takes energy. Your brain, your subconscious, the three voices—they don't want you to use that part of the brain to conserve that energy.

You see, the brain's core goal is your survival, and it doesn't like the idea of you wasting energy on a silly task like "thinking" when, according to its original wiring, at any point, a saber-toothed tiger could jump in your window.

When it came to the second question, when I asked you to solve the equation, you could have gotten pen and paper. You could have started solving it, but your brain said, "No, what if a saber-tooth tiger comes in the window and tries to eat you in the middle of doing it?"

That's the ancient human survival instinct. The survival mode that kicks in within your brain, that's all it cares about. The survival mode says, "Don't waste energy. You only ate a little bit of food this morning for breakfast. You don't have much energy left."

Your brain is concerned that if you've got to run from a predator, you need to save energy. It doesn't want you to engage the active part of your brain.

So, you go through life in passive mode.

You can tell you're in passive mode because of the answer to the first question.

You didn't just answer it, even if you didn't write it down. You probably had an answer appear in your mind, but your brain invented that figure. It made it up because it didn't know the answer without checking (not that the negative voice would have allowed you to Google it).

Your brain thought it was a simple answer to make up because it knew no one would check it. That's the passive mode. It makes things up. It doesn't actually know because you didn't actually think about it.

Your brain didn't try and calculate it or reason it out. The three voices answered, "It's probably this, whatever." They thought you could get by with any vaguely correct answer because no one was going to check.

However, the minute it had to solve an actual equation, your voices didn't have an answer. They didn't want to try and guess because they knew the guess would be wrong.

Just like your brain wants to protect you from losing energy, it also wants to protect you from feeling like it's wrong. It doesn't want you to feel bad.

That's that negative voice. Negative voice is like, "You can't solve that. That's too difficult. Don't look stupid. Just say lots. You know you could solve this if you wanted to. It doesn't matter. No one is going to be upset with you."

That's the negative voice taking control of your brain.

You weren't actively controlling your ship. If you were active, if you were really active, if you were Warren Buffett, if you were Tony Robbins, your active brain, the true fan, would have said, "You can solve this. Get a pen and paper out. Start doing some long multiplication, or grab your calculator, it's on your phone."

Prove that you can do it yourself. Do it now.

Heck, even if you did it afterward, you just learned how to engage your active brain. It takes effort, more effort than you think it's worth. Correction, more effort than the negative voice in your brain thinks it's worth. It takes energy to keep the active part of your brain engaged, a lot of energy.

Have you ever been trying to solve a problem at work or maybe trying to solve a complicated puzzle or even a video game and you start rubbing the top of your head? Or you try to concentrate, and you find yourself rubbing the sides of your forehead? You may even get that headache at the front of your head. It's because you're thinking so much.

If you've ever experienced this, it's simply because that is where you feel pain from the cerebral cortex. It lives in the outermost part of your brain. So, when you're engaging it when you're using it, it's tiring. It takes energy, and after a while, you can't really do it anymore, and you shift back to passive mode.

But the point is...you *can* control it. You can think back to the ship. You've got your own ship, and you're the captain. You can't sail it the whole time. You have to go into passive mode occasionally. You have to rest, take time to recover; you have to be able to relax, and you do that by shifting back into passive mode every so often.

The problem is, what happens when you drop back into passive mode and you don't have the three voices programmed to do what you want them to?

If you don't have the war over the inner monologue sorted out, your negative voice wins every time. It's like you're piloting your ship. You're the captain, and suddenly you say, "You know what, guys? I've got to go to sleep. I have been actively engaged in this journey the whole time, and I've got to get some rest."

So, you lay down to sleep, and the negative voice takes over: "Whoa! How can we cripple this success? Let's turn around. There's no point going there. That's the wrong place." You end up miles off course, and you wake up in the morning, and you're thinking, "Why am I over here?"

The negative voice says, "Well, I decided that seeing as how you're going to fail anyway, I thought I'd take us home."

Have you ever had that happen in your life? Have you ever started succeeding and then you started to fail? You know it's self-sabotage; you just don't know why it keeps happening.

This is the most important point for you to understand. You can actively control that negative voice, but eventually when you're tired, when everything starts to get you down when you have some bad experiences, the passive mode will kick in and then that negative voice will appear.

And it's all because of your survival instinct.

Next Steps: Now, I've been talking about ships a lot throughout this chapter. Because of that, I want to invite you to a unique experience that I currently have in the works. How would you like to spend a week with me, working one-on-one to shake you out of passive mode and getting that negative voice to shut up...while also cruising across the Atlantic Ocean? For the first time, I'm offering a "Working Vacation" cruise dedicated to helping you with any negativity or other problems you may have. In my experience, there's nothing better for curing negativity than taking a break from work, and sipping margaritas while soaking up the sun.

So, check out this link to see how you can enjoy the sunshine while learning how to shift gears into active mode: PsychologyHacker.com/Cruise

Chapter 4: How Your Survival Instinct Shapes Your Subconscious

So far, we've discussed how your subconscious has three voices. One of them is that negative voice that tells you that you're going to fail.

I'm still taking you through understanding how your brain works, and now you're going to learn how to kill that negative voice.

The second voice is the true fan. The true fan wants you to succeed in life. It's like, "You can do this. You can make it happen." The negative voice and the true fan are at war all the time. They're fighting for control of your subconscious decisions.

The third and final voice is the mentor. The mentor is capable of siding with either one, but for most people, it usually ends up siding with the negative voice due to a history of negative experiences.

The mentor's voice looks at what's happened in your life. It looks at your experiences and says to the negative voice, "You know what? Experience and history say you're usually right, so I'm going to side with you."

The two voices then overpower your true fan.

You, the real you, you're capable of being in control. You can actively engage your brain, and you can shut down those three voices and say, "I don't care which choice you want to make. I'm going to do the work anyway."

It takes a lot of energy to use the active brain, and eventually, most of us slip back into that passive brain, with our subconscious making most of our daily decisions for us.

By now you should realize that if you can kill that negative voice if you can make it go away even when you're in passive mode, you'll still be succeeding.

You will be pushing all you can in active mode, and then you will still choose to succeed and push on when you're in passive mode! You're still succeeding because the negative voice is literally nowhere to be seen.

But before you can go about killing your negative voice, you need to understand survival mode because this is very important.

Survival mode is incredibly powerful, as it has the power to automatically engage your three subconscious voices and shut off the active part of your brain.

There's a very good reason for this. We've upgraded our predator to a twenty-first-century model, but the underlying principle remains...

When a lion jumps into your room and is trying to eat you, it is incredibly important that you don't sit there and engage the active brain. As we discussed earlier, the active part of your brain takes energy and, more importantly, the active brain is slow.

The answer to the first question in the previous chapter probably just appeared in your mind. That's because, as we've discussed, your subconscious gave you the answer before it attempted to make an educated guess, so no calculations were necessary.

But calculating an answer takes more energy because you're using that cortex part of your brain. The more you have to think about something, and if you sat down with a pen and paper and tried to calculate that equation, for instance, it would take energy, and it would take time.

If you've got to solve a problem and that problem is life or death, then you've got an issue because you don't have time, and your brain definitely doesn't want you wasting energy that you may need to fight or run.

So, the brain doesn't give you a choice. The minute you enter into survival mode, the brain shuts off the active brain. You don't have a say anymore. You're living on instinct.

Now you've probably heard this before. Whenever a fierce situation arises, whenever something bad happens, maybe a lion jumps into the room or you're about to talk to someone you're attracted to, and you're nervous, or you're going to ask your boss for a promotion, or you're going for an interview, the minute you get that "Arghh my heart is pounding, I'm nervous. There are butterflies in my stomach" feeling; you're in survival mode. The brain says to you, "No active brain for you. We're not going to calculate anything. We're going to trust the subconscious to make snap decisions."

What happens is you get that fight, flight, or freeze instinct. You've probably heard about those three instincts that take control during stressful situations.

Those three instincts are going to take over, and they're going to tell you what to do. Your three instincts are not the same as the three voices. They're very simple. The three instincts are more like different plans of action. When you're in trouble, your brain will default to one of these three action plans.

The three voices aren't out of the picture, however. When you're in survival mode, they will choose which instinct action plan you're going to follow. They get to pick and choose.

And they always pick the same way.

They always pick what helped you out the last time.

So, if you ran away the last time you dealt with a scary situation, you're going to run away next time. This is why people who are scared of going for a new job or a promotion never go for it. Or people who are scared of talking to people they're attracted to never get the confidence.

The minute you get nervous, survival mode kicks in, and once you're in survival mode, only the three voices get a say. If you ran away last time, you can be sure the negative voice will say, "You're going to fail." So, you will avoid the fear-triggering situation and run again.

The active brain doesn't get to overrule anything when survival mode is engaged. And the minute the active brain gets switched off, the decision has already been made. It defaults to the same decision as last time because that's the fastest thing to do.

Logically this makes sense. The fastest thing to do is whatever worked last time.

And if you survived the situation, your brain considers it a successful tactic and chooses to do it the next time, and time and time again.

This is where the pattern of failure kicks in. The negative voice has full control whenever you're in survival mode.

The first time a lion jumps into your room and tries to kill you, your active brain switches off, and the three voices begin to make a decision:

"Okay, what are we going to do?"

The true fan says, "We can take this lion. Let's take it out and kill it."

The negative voice responds, "No way. We're going to fail. We're never going to succeed."

The mentor looks at previous situations. Except in this situation, it doesn't have a point of reference, as no lions have ever entered your room before. In that case, it looks at the closest similar situation, and when it comes to danger, that's typically going to be run, or indecision...which is to freeze and do nothing.

After all, if the true fan and the negative voice are in a stalemate, and the mentor can't add anything to the discussion, you'll be frozen. As the saying goes: frozen with fear.

This means that for any situation you're unfamiliar with, your default is often a negative one. To either do nothing (freeze up) or to avoid it by running away, which would be the negative voice's choice.

As I said, if most of the time you make negative choices, the negative voice is going to win more often, and the mentor will default to siding with your negative voice more and more.

That probably sounds great to you right now. You're probably thinking, *you know what? If the lion jumps in, I want to run away.*

That's why the negative voice exists.

When lions were jumping in people's bedrooms, you needed that negative voice to get you out. I don't know about you, but lions don't often jump into my bedroom.

Actually, that's not true. I have four kids, and my last name is Lyons, so technically lions do jump into my bedroom all the time. But this is my point. The lions that come into my bedroom nowadays aren't trying to rip me to shreds. They're my kids. They're playing a game. They're pretending to be lions. They're trying to scare me.

If my negative voice won and I responded with, "Oh my! Oh no! The kids need to stop running into my room trying to scare me," then I would just look weak and not be a solid father figure for my children to look up to.

These dangerous situations aren't common anymore. The negative voice is more often than not plain wrong because of this. It's not needed anymore. You don't need it to hold you back.

When my survival mode kicks in, I can't access my active brain. I can't think, *hmm, is that a real lion or is that just my kid in a really good costume?* I can't think like that because the active brain is off. But I don't want to be scared of my child running into my room. I don't need that fear anymore.

On the other hand, I do need the true fan. I need the true fan to take control of my survival instinct situations. I need it to tell me, "You know what? You've got this. If it is a lion, who cares? You're going to stand in front of the lion and protect your family. You're going to be a strong, protective parent. You're going to face that challenge and deal with it."

I need the true fan to tell me I can deal with that situation because it isn't a lion.

You know what it could be, though? It could be somebody breaking into my house. It could be somebody trying to hurt my family.

But again, if the negative voice wins, I dart straight out the door and I leave my family in that situation. Not cool.

I want the true fan to kick in. Deal with the assailant. Deal with the threat. Deal with the person who broke into my house, so my family can run away and be safe. That's what I need to happen. I need the true fan to help me fight back.

As you've probably realized by now, the solution isn't found in the negative voice. The real issue is the mentor. In a situation that I've never dealt with before, the mentor doesn't know what to do. If most of the time I'm negative, then I'm going to default to that same flight response. I'm going to run away. I'm not going to take the fight response; I'm not going to take the right action to succeed.

What's worse is that in situations where the true fan and the negative voice don't know what to do, the mentor has to take over and make a choice.

As explained above, if the mentor has no experience with the situation or no history of decisions to fall back on, then the decision will be to do nothing.

Worse, if that decision kept you alive, then you will always do nothing.

Now, I want you to imagine that you're going for a job promotion. Naturally, you're going to feel nervous. What sucks is that that nervous feeling can trigger survival mode, because your body can't tell the difference between the fear of a new job interview and the fear of being eaten by a lion. Chemically your brain can't tell the difference.

It's not like we went to job interviews 50,000 years ago. When we're faced with any kind of threat, the human brain reverts to survival mode, which is not necessarily helpful for job interviews!

You're either in survival mode, or you're not in survival mode. When you're in survival mode, the active brain is gone. So, in survival mode, it all comes down to the voices to make a choice.

I want you to look at the options. You've got the true fan, saying, "We can do this. Let's take the action step." It's encouraging and positive.

The other two options are discouraging and negative: "Don't do anything because we don't have a reference of what to do," or "Let's run away from it because it will end badly if we don't." Either of those two action plans will stop you from succeeding. If you listen to either one, the result will be the same: You don't get the job. You don't get the promotion. You don't start your business. You don't move out from the terrible situation you're in.

You need the true fan to win. You need the true fan to be engaged when you're in passive mode, and you need the true fan to be engaged when you're in survival mode. It has to happen.

As the captain of your ship, your brain just can't take control when you're in survival mode because it's going to make quick decisions. It can't sit there and work out whether a lion is real or fake. While you're trying to work out if it is real, it kills you. You don't have the luxury of time.

I'll give another example. Imagine I get a knife, and I throw it at your head. Now you've got three options. You can dodge out of the way, which would equate to running away (flight). You can try to curl up and protect yourself if the knife hits you anyway, which is to do nothing (freeze). Or you can catch it and throw it back at me, which would be to take action (fight).

Again, you're going to do what you've done before, so most people are going to run away if they're used to dodging things, or they're going to stand there and do nothing and get hit if they have no idea what to do.

But if they've trained in martial arts, or juggling or something similar, they're going to catch it and throw it back at me. That would be the active choice.

Now, here's what you *don't* want to do. The biggest thing that you mustn't do is try to work out whether the knife is real or not. You can't have the active brain engaged and think, *I wonder if that's a real knife or a fake knife*?

You can't let that happen. You have to trust survival mode to keep you alive.

Survival mode is going to do exactly what you want. Once again, we see that in our hypothetical life-or-death situations, it's okay to have the plan of running away. That's a perfectly reasonable option.

This is why it's important to understand how your brain makes decisions. When you understand how it operates, you can hack your brain to give you success.

More often than not, the negative voice is wrong. Thankfully, people don't just go around throwing knives at other people anymore. But if we did, and if I had to deal with a situation where people were throwing knives at me all the time, I'd want to be able to catch them and throw them back.

So, what would I do? I would train. I would practice. I would give people fake knives. I'd say, "Throw that knife at me so I can catch it and throw it back at you."

If people were throwing knives at random people, then I wouldn't be the guy thinking *I'm going to run away and dodge knives because one day I'm going to fail to escape or dodge.* I want to be the guy who catches the knife and throws it back, so people are scared.

They won't want to throw knives at me. I want people thinking, *don't throw knives at that guy. He throws them back at you, and it hurts.*

Once again, the true fan wins. You need the true fan to be engaged to succeed. I have seen this in my own life numerous times and in the lives of all my clients.

Next Steps: If you'd like to see how some of my students have been able to invigorate their true fan, I would highly suggest taking a look at the Facebook page for Psychology Hackers. My students will often share stories of how their true fan let them push through and achieve success they would never have been able to before. Check out the link below to see how well things have worked out for my students, as well as a few tips on how to make the same thing work for you! Facebook.com/PsychologyHacker

Chapter 5: How Your Negative Voice Can Keep You Trapped in a Bad Situation

I mentioned earlier in the book about a time in my life when my negative voice affected me in a really bad way. This happened years ago, long before I was voted the number one dating coach in the world, long before I was financially successful and had the life I lead now.

I was in a relationship with a girl, and the reason I was in this relationship was probably one of the worst reasons to date anyone. I dated her because I didn't think girls liked me.

When I was in school, I was never particularly big physically. My father used to joke that my arms were like sparrows' kneecaps. Possibly because of this, possibly for other reasons, the result was that I was bullied. But specifically, I was bullied by girls. They would kick me, lock me in the closet, and call me horrible names. They would tell me I was least likely ever to get a girlfriend.

In fact, that particular phrase was attributed to me by my entire class of 38 students.

They wrote it on a board next to my name and voted on it. Repeating over and over that I'd never get a girlfriend. That stuck. It stuck hard. I believed it. It trained my internal mentor to believe that I would never have a girlfriend, and my negative voice took hold. I held on to that for years. It started when I was 15 years old, and I'd had no experience with girls before that point.

From 15 to 25, if I could get a girl to even look at me, I'd basically beg her to date me. We didn't have Facebook back then, but if we did, I'm sure I would've been the guy who would have messaged people's profiles saying, "Oh, my God, I would love to have a girl like you. I'd treat you well. I'd love to hang out with you." Or, "Please, can you hang out with me?" Or, "I'll do anything for you." I'm sure I would have been that guy, safely expressing my desires and wishes behind the comfort of a computer screen.

It's not because I was horrible or weird. It was because I didn't know what to do in real life. But, whenever a situation came up where I was actually hanging out with a girl, I never had the confidence to make a physical move. I never went for a kiss; I never went to have sex. I froze, or I ran away. I didn't have the confidence to interact normally with girls in person.

So, when I finally got a girl who thought, I *like this guy running around and doing things for me, I'll stay with him,* I loved it and was so excited.

In my head, it was like the curse was broken. *I had a girlfriend!* I remember being so happy about it. I was so happy I didn't stop to think whether I *should* date her. I was blind to signs of trouble that most normal guys would have noticed right away.

For instance, she suggested I pay all the bills. I simply thought, *whatever, that's what a real man does; we pay all the bills.*

Due to that thought process, I paid all the bills, every single one of them, for the entire year we were together. Meanwhile, she was working. She would take her money and keep it. I literally had no money because I was giving her every dollar I earned because that's the "manly" thing to do. She saved her money and with it, bought a house. She bought a brand-new Toyota RAV4 when I couldn't even afford to get driving lessons because I was paying all our bills. The car and house were in her name. Everything was hers and I, well, I had nothing.

What happened next shouldn't have been a surprise, but back then it was. After nine months of dating her, I found out she was cheating on me. She would go out in the evenings with her friends and her money, and she would hang out with other guys. I didn't do anything. I didn't say anything. I didn't react at all because I didn't want to lose my girlfriend.

The negative voice inside my head told me that I wouldn't be able to get another woman to date me, and even if she wasn't treating me the best, at least I wasn't alone. My reasoning was, "At least my friends think I have a girlfriend and therefore I'm not the biggest loser when it comes to women anymore. I'm not the least likely person to ever get a girlfriend because I'm dating someone, even if she's not nice to me."

It got so bad I would spend my evenings sitting alone inside my house and not hanging out with my friends. I didn't want them to see that I was all alone because she was going out with other guys.

This was back in 2006 before I became an expert in attraction, and it was awful. I'll never forget the one day she came home and said, "You know what? I can't do this anymore. I don't like being with you. I'm going to leave you." And she left.

I went to work that day, and I was devastated. I called my friend and told him, "I think we're breaking up. I think she's leaving. She wants to come by the house today and pick up her stuff."

I remember thinking I couldn't bear to see her. (Once again, my three voices were convincing me to avoid a situation I didn't want to deal with.) I remember asking my friend, "Would you mind staying in the house? I'm at work all day, and I'd like someone there while she gets her stuff."

My friend agreed and stayed at my house for the day while I went off to work. I didn't think much about her being at the house. I was focused on work, and I barely noted the fact that my friend texted me to confirm that she had collected her stuff.

When I came home that night (remember I'd hidden from *all* my friends, the fact that my relationship was terrible), I noticed that my entire apartment, everything in it, had been wrecked. She took everything. She took my PlayStation. She took my PC. She took my video games. She took the fucking shower curtain! It was that bad. She took everything. These were things that were mine.

I looked at my friend, and I said, "Dude, why did you let her take everything?"

He responded, "Man, she came in with some other guy. They were laughing and making out. They were playing around in the bedroom and jumping on the bed. They were taking everything. What was I going to do? The guy was huge. He was big, man. I just let them take...I didn't know what was yours. I didn't know what was hers."

I'll never forget the way he looked at me. He was in shock. I couldn't blame him. Until the day before, as far as he knew my relationship had been perfect.

There it was, one of my best friends looking at this girl who was supposed to be my girlfriend making out with some other guy in my apartment, taking everything back to her house that she bought with her savings while I had been paying for our entire lifestyle, and I had nothing. I had no money to replace anything. That's when I hit rock bottom.

My friends talked about me behind my back. They all thought things like *you're a loser, dude. Women will never want you.*

The fact is, though, they didn't say it to me; they thought it. I was sure of it. Every single time I looked at them, I felt horrible. Ashamed. Unworthy. I was providing evidence to my internal mentor, and these negative experiences were shaping my future decisions even then.

That's what the mentor does. The mentor in your brain can't create new ideas. It can't come up with awesome or even terrible things. It just looks at your experiences, and it uses them to make decisions. That's why the mentor can side with the negative voice so often. If you experience negative things, your subconscious will make the decision to protect you from those things in the future. It will decide to help you avoid pain, emotional or physical.

This is what happens. When you have a bad situation like the one I described, the mentor thinks, *wow, this is what happens if you date somebody so you probably shouldn't date anybody.* Or, *remember that time you went for that job interview and you didn't get it? Well, why bother applying for this other job?*

For most of us, our mentor starts learning things when we're still children. It's funny; if you look at any child when they're a baby, they're more often than not born an extrovert. Newborn babies aren't ashamed to be themselves. They want to interact with people.

When I had my third child, right after he was born, I noticed he stared at strangers and smiled. Actually, technically he made faces at them. He'd look at me, too, make a face, and I would make a face back at him, and he would think it was the funniest thing ever.

That's what kids do. They engage with other people, while we, as adults, tell them to stop it because we're embarrassed. We say, "Stop making that noise. Stop talking to a stranger. Don't bother that person. You don't know who they are. Something bad can happen." We're protective. We get used to telling kids, "No, don't do this. Don't do that."

We think we're protecting them but what we're actually doing is teaching their mentor to say no. We're giving our children's mentor these negative experiences, and their mentor remembers. That's what the mentor is designed to do. The mentor has a long memory, and it collects things like: "Don't talk to strangers." "Don't put yourself in a situation where you could fail." "Don't go for that goal because it's not going to work."

As much as it hurts, this is what your parents did to you.

Here's a common situation: Did you ever want to start a sport, or a hobby and your parents asked you, "Will you stick with it? Will you actually do it?"

Most children will respond, "I don't know."

Well, most children don't know because the voices in their subconscious don't know what to say. Yet your parents may have said, "Well, if you're not going to stick with it, you shouldn't do it."

Faced with that, a child may think, *well I don't know if I will, so maybe they're right; maybe I shouldn't.*

That negative voice gains all that momentum. As you get older, the negative voice wins because most of us have parents who told us (and who continue to tell us) don't do this; don't do that. They're filling your mentor with all of these "don't do it" voices.

Don't do it. You're going to fail.

It's not just your parents. As you start to default to avoiding and taking the negative option, your own bad experiences and decisions will continue to shape your mentor as well.

But the opposite is also true. If you've known someone growing up who is now super successful, it's often because their parents were incredibly supportive, telling them, "You can do this. You can do that. You can be great." When they were little, they would have tried out for football or something else and beat everybody.

The irony is that often they weren't even trying to beat "everybody." Why? Simply because not everybody entered. "Everybody" didn't feel they had a chance. The people who defaulted to the fact they will probably fail didn't even show up. Because "everybody" isn't there, it becomes a lot easier for the positive people to win.

These positive experiences shape their mentor, too, encouraging them to try more and more scenarios where others think they will fail. And they succeed more and more. Not all the time, but each success encourages them to try more.

Sometimes these successful people can appear arrogant, not because they are, but because they don't have the negative voice telling them they're going to fail. They just know how to succeed because they always have, and life actually is easier for them. They don't have to overcome the negative voice and waste energy fighting themselves. They can focus on only achieving success.

That's what our goal is here at the institute. We want to give you that same ability. We want to unlock that mentor that works *with* you to create your success, even if you're just coasting through life in passive mode.

The good news is when you get this, you're not going to come off as arrogant because you've had the experience of that negative voice in your head holding you back. Even if you become amazing, the experiences and the memory of those negative experiences don't ever truly leave so you won't appear arrogant. Instead, you will just build your true fan up to be awesome, and you'll know that you can succeed.

Remember, your mentor also has all these positive experiences that can help you. It can swing your true fan to victory. The negative voice is still there, but it's a lot quieter. But, you're not arrogant. You're not shoving your success in people's faces. No, you *are* succeeding.

Next Steps: Quieting down that negative voice in your head, and embracing a more positive outlook, is one of the biggest changes you can make that will ensure your success both in business and in life. Click this link to check out one of my daily videos, where I discuss all aspects of success and positivity. For this particular video, I discuss this one small vocabulary trick that can supercharge your true fan. Check it out! Be sure to check out the rest of my daily videos as well; they're all very short and get right to the point when it comes to providing useful advice. Here's that link: PsychologyHacker.com/Language

Chapter 6: How I Trained My Mentor for Success

That dating experience was a negative one for me. I hit rock bottom. I remember thinking, I *don't know what I'm going to do with my life. Girls don't like me. The girl that was cheating on me still decided to leave me and worse; she took everything. I've got no TV, no computer, no furniture, no money, and I don't know what to do.*

That's when I met this crazy Viking. He was this guy in London back in the day who was known as a dating expert. He'd studied under experts in the field like Neil Strauss, who I mentioned earlier and is one of the best dating experts in the world. But this Viking didn't merely study dating. He studied success.

This Viking was a crazy Danish guy. I heard about him through some friends who suggested that he might be able to solve my dating problem. It took weeks to track him down. I was nervous; I was terrified, but I told him I wanted to learn from him.

I wanted him to be my mentor—not the mentor in my head, but my real mentor. I wanted him to show me what to do.

He told me, "You know what? It's going to cost you $20,000."

I nearly choked. I didn't have that kind of money. I stared at him for what felt like hours.

Finally, I responded, "I don't have that kind of money, but I would love to come and work with you."

He simply said, "Find the money, and we'll do it."

Then I looked at my finances and realized since I was no longer paying so much to a girl who didn't want to date me, I could probably repurpose my income and pay him in monthly installments, and he would work with me over a period of time.

This was the first time I'd ever hired a "success coach." Today I have three or four at any given time. I have a coach for martial arts, a coach for health, a coach for diet, a coach for financial advice, for business strategy and more.

Because once you realize the benefits you get from a mentor and how they can shape the way your internal mentor operates, it's like going through life on "God mode" where whatever you want can happen.

As crazy as this sounds, it really is that easy. Suddenly the internal conflict in your head is gone...you just do the things you need to do, to get the success you want. You can even do it in passive mode, with your mentor and true fan carrying your decisions the way you need them to be taken.

While working with that crazy Viking, the mentor in my head was suddenly witnessing and hearing all these amazing things that could be done, and it started to reform the way it made decisions. It could see that certain choices brought better results than it thought possible.

I saw people walking up to women in the street, getting their phone numbers, going on dates with them, and it was obvious the women were happy about it.

These situations completely transformed the way my mentor made decisions. My old thoughts were shattered as this Viking began to reform my internal mentor.

I wish I'd known much earlier how easy it could've been to improve my life. I was so depressed, so sad. Back in 2006, I was just this guy who'd lost his girlfriend, had no money in the bank, had no belongings, didn't even have a computer; I was this guy who'd lost absolutely everything.

I wish someone had explained to me about the negative voice in my head that was holding me back. That all I had to do was find someone to build up my internal mentor, to give me these positive experiences and show me what was possible and help to guide me, educating my mentor into making the correct decisions. If I'd had all that, my negative voice wouldn't be able to control me anymore.

The fact is that with just a little guidance, my internal mentor completely transformed. Because that's what it's designed to do!

The mentor in my head would hear and see the crazy Viking and all the other mentors who worked with me. So, when my true fan said, "You can do this," the mentor in my head would start referencing the mentors in my life. It would say, "Yeah, you know what? You can do it because we saw this other guy do this before." Or, "If you take these three steps, you'll end up being able to do it."

This is when the mentor suddenly sides with the true fan, and you can do anything. I mean literally anything.

I mentioned before that I went from being a lost cause in dating to becoming known as one of the leading dating coaches in the world. But that's not the only successful business I own. I also run a film company, and we've had shows on the Discovery Channel and have even made a unique original series for Yahoo. The success from that helped me buy myself a really nice family car, a Mercedes.

As I said before, I grew up poor. I couldn't even afford driving lessons, let alone a car. I was so poor back then I couldn't do anything that cost money, yet there I was buying my family a Mercedes.

That's not our only car. From the success of my other company, I also bought myself a Maserati. I'm not saying this to brag. I'm saying it to show you that you can achieve *anything*.

I went from no money, no dating life, to living a crazy lifestyle with everything I could ever dream of, and it's all because I killed that negative voice inside my head by training my mentor.

Once I started hanging out with that crazy Viking, going around and doing all these awesome things, I found that it's possible to attract not just one woman but even two women at once. I remember there was this beautiful moment within six months of my girlfriend breaking up with me. I was walking down the street, and I had two girls, one on each arm. I had just left the nightclub with both of them. My old girlfriend saw me in the street and said, "Oh really, so this is your life now?"

I remember thinking, *wow! She saw me on the street, and she's jealous of the fact that I have these two girls.*

I also learned that it is possible to have a relationship with multiple women. Over the last few years, the story of my two girlfriends and I has gone viral. We've been featured on Steve Harvey's show, on LADbible, and on countless news stations.

I've been living with both of them for almost four years now. I'm not saying you should date multiple people. I'm saying *anything* is possible. I live in a world where I have two girlfriends because my true fan says it's possible. It says, "Yeah, you can have two girlfriends because I've seen it. I know it's possible."

I don't have a negative voice telling me that it can't happen because now I've done it. I've had incredible experiences financially. I've had incredible experiences in my love life, and that's translated into incredible improvements in my health as well.

After my second son was born, I weighed 205 pounds. A blood test revealed some issues, and my doctor said my health was in danger. I was considered technically "obese," yet 14 weeks later I got my body weight down to 171 and increased my muscle mass significantly.

I completely changed my body. I just woke up one day and said, "You know what? I'm going to change my body." The true fan was like, "Yeah, you can do it. You can make it happen." The negative voice said, "You're going to fail. You're never going to do it." The mentor had all the voices of experience from my recent past and the people around me, and it sided with my true fan.

I simply phoned up two or three people who I knew were experts in fitness, and I sat on the phone with them for a few hours and had them tell me all the things I needed to do. I had action steps, and I was prepared for my negative voice to tell me, "You can't do it." When that happened, I looked at the piece of paper in front of me and thought, *you know what, negative voice? You are wrong.*

I let my active brain and the mentor take over and suddenly thought, *look, there is a 10-step plan here. If I follow this every single week, it's going to work. I know it's going to work because it worked for other people. Their lives changed. Not just their lives, but their students' lives changed, too. My entire life will change because of these steps. I just have to follow them, and I'm going to get the result I want.* That's called experience.

When my negative voice said, "But what if you fail?" the mentor replied, "Well, no one else failed. They just kept doing it." The true fan piped in, "Yeah, just do it." The negative voice had no choice but to think, *oh well, I gave my opinion.*

In truth, nowadays I tend to control my negative voice with phrases like, "That's right, you gave your opinion, and no one fucking cares. No one cares what you have to say, negative voice, because you're wrong. Because if I take steps that are proven to work that other people have taken, then it's going to work."

Don't forget how the mentor works. When you're young, and someone tells you something may fail, the mentor "knows" that the experience is likely to fail so then you're going to fail. Your mentor makes its decisions based on what it sees, what it hears, and what it learns.

But the beautiful thing about the mentor is that if your active brain is engaged, you can rewrite it. You can teach it, "Look, these are the steps. Here's the evidence that it worked."

I am living proof that you can go from living on the wrong side of the tracks with no money growing up, that you can be in a terrible relationship where someone cheats on you, and you pay for absolutely everything, to living in a $1.5 million home right on the beach in California, or on a 44-acre ranch in Texas. That you can drive a Maserati and a Mercedes, and you can live in a house with your two girlfriends and have a threesome every single day. That's the life that I lead today.

Above all, better than any of that, I have four wonderful children. I get to spend every single day playing with them. I'm watching them grow up and grow old, and I have time for them because I run my own business. I make my own money. I do all of this because the true fan is behind me, and my mentor is not built out of my causal experiences but is built out of the experiences I have allowed myself to take in, to adopt, by making sure that I am working with exceptional people who are giving me a full breakdown of exactly what to do.

Next Steps: As you can guess from my experiences learning from The Viking, an actual mentor can do wonders for building up the experiences and decisions that a mental mentor needs to make. Knowing someone who's been through it all before, and who's got all the answers, is one of the most reassuring things I know of. Because of that, I'd like to offer you an opportunity to work directly with me!

Click the link to check out the various coaching plans I offer! All can be customized to your exact needs! Just go here: PsychologyHacker.com/Coaching

Chapter 7: Positivity Hacks

If my dad were sitting here right now, he'd be telling you that the reason I'm so successful in life, is that: "My son's just lucky."

But the truth is, I don't believe in luck, and in fact, not only do I not believe in luck, but a lot of very famous and successful psychologists also don't believe in luck. You see, the truth is, in my opinion, luck comes down to two factors. It is preparation meeting opportunity. If you are prepared for success, then when an opportunity comes along, you can jump on that opportunity and be successful.

To the casual observer, it looks like you got lucky because a random opportunity came by and you just happened to have the skill set to jump on it and take advantage of it. But the truth is, that the time and the effort you put into getting prepared, is actually what enabled you to take up that opportunity.

Opportunities come up all the time. Every time you meet somebody you're getting a new opportunity. Every time you talk to someone about their business, every time you read an advert, every time you meet somebody who owns a big business and they're struggling, it's an opportunity for you to help them. There are a lot of opportunities out there, the trick to being luckier and being more successful is being prepared for them. And the key to positivity and to hacking your own positivity and the psychology behind it is to make sure that you're prepared.

There is an awesome psychological study done on luck and the power of positivity. In the experiment, two groups of people were used, one identified themselves as being primarily positive and optimistic, and another group thought of themselves as negative. Both these groups were instructed to count how many pictures were inside a magazine, and they were to time how long it took them to do it. On average, the people that considered themselves optimistic would complete the task ridiculously fast, like 10 times faster than the people who were negative about it.

It all has to do with the way people approach tasks and life, on whether they are positive or negative people. You see what happened is the negative people would dread the task, and the idea of looking through a magazine and counting every single picture sounded absolutely horrible to them. But the positive people were kind of enjoying it; they were going through reading the articles and relishing the task because they felt positive about it.

That meant that the positive people, who put their time into focusing on actually reading the magazine, saw an advert earlier on in the magazine that said, "Contestants taking part in this study, just so you know, there are X pictures in the magazine. You do not need to read the magazine. You can hand it in."

What was completely shocking about this is all the negative people failed to spot that advert in the middle of the magazine. Even though they went through the task and looked at the magazine, they didn't see it because they were so caught up in their negativity.

The psychologist who conducted this experiment was Richard Wiseman. The question is how did he know that some people weren't just lucky? How did he know it was positivity versus negativity? Well, that's because later on in the magazine there was another advert that said: "Participants, if you see this when you hand it in, show it to the psychologist, and you'll receive a cash prize." No one got the cash prize.

If the positive people had been lucky, they would've gone through it, seen the later note, and would've claimed the cash prize. But they didn't, because they saw the first one that said you don't have to complete the study; you can hand it in. The reason that they seemed to be "lucky" was because they were positive and enjoyed the experience. Because they were enjoying it they were actually paying attention to what they were doing; they were prepared for the opportunity, and they came up and took it and finished the task early. They weren't lucky, because if they were lucky, they would have randomly found the right page and gotten the money.

The negative people didn't see either of the two adverts inside the magazine and instead, they counted every single one and took ages to do it. So, positivity and negativity can drastically affect your life. If you identify as being somebody who's negative, it's going to stop you from being successful. You're not going to take risks, because you're not going to believe it's going to work. You're not going to try new endeavors, because after all they're bound to fail.

If you're someone who's positive, you are going to be ready for opportunities. You are going to learn new things, and you're going to be more prepared for success.

But, how do you become positive? How do you cultivate that positivity? Well, it comes down to two key factors, and if I were going to give you a psychological hack to become more positive, it'd be focusing on these two pieces. The first part is that you want to stop talking negatively about yourself; don't put yourself down; don't say negative things about yourself. Take your time and enjoy every single task you do. Even if a task looks like it's going to suck, don't complain about it. Don't be negative about it. Don't be like "This is going to suck for me," or "I'm going to hate it," or "I'm going to suck at it." Because all of those things become affirmations, where you tell yourself you suck; you tell yourself you're negative, and then the situation becomes negative. When this happens, you're not actually prepared for any success that could come out of the particular circumstance.

Again, the first element is making sure you're controlling your mind and making sure it's only thinking positive things about you versus negative things. Rather than just trying to say positive things about yourself, try not to say negative things. Instead, try to slow down and enjoy every single task you do and see the positive in the situation.

Now, there is one thing that's going to make that very difficult to do, and that is negative people. This is probably the hardest piece of advice I'll have to give you. If somebody in your life is habitually negative, you really need to stop spending as much time around them. The reason for this is simple. If you put your positive energy into helping somebody else, while that may seem noble, they are only going to see the negative in what you're doing.

You've probably experienced this yourself, where you try and help somebody who feels negative, and yet they still complain about it. Then you feel bad because you're putting in energy to try and help them, and they don't appreciate it. The truth is, if they're negative, they can't appreciate it, because they're negative, and they can only see the negativity. They're not prepared to receive positivity, so therefore, they can't see it. But your effort is going to take energy away from you; it is going to make you feel that there's no point putting in positive effort for anyone because it's not appreciated. That's going to make you less likely to give positive effort anywhere else.

The best place to place positive energy is into yourself, and into other positive people. When you put positive energy into positive people, they appreciate it. They're prepared and welcome receiving it. They reciprocate. They give you positive energy. They help you succeed, and that cultivates a more positive persona.

There is nothing, *nothing* that will change your outlook on life more than only hanging around positive people. If you don't believe me if you're struggling with this, or you think that the negative people in your life are holding you back, but you can't separate from them, go on vacation. Take an extended vacation for a couple of weeks. But don't take friends, don't take family, don't take anyone who's negative. Instead, focus on meeting new people. Look for the happiest, friendliest people, and try and add value to their lives. Try and make them have fun, try and make them enjoy their experience more.

When you help positive people enjoy their experience more, they are going to make sure that you enjoy your experience more. Ultimately that's what you need. If you really want to make sure that you're a positive person, then you've got to make sure that you're not negative about yourself and you're spending less time with negative people.

I'm not saying spend no time; I'm not saying cut them out of your life, just less time, and know that when you are around them, they're going to drain that positivity out of you. So, you need to make sure you balance it by spending time with positive people as well.

This is something I consciously make sure I'm doing. If I spend an amount of time with negative people, I know I have to go away then and spend time with positive people, to replenish my positive energy.

But even if you're trying to do this, there are a couple of obstacles that could hold you back from being successful in those areas. One, of course, is if you're struggling to network. If you don't know how to network with strangers, or you don't have great networking skills, or you don't know how to talk to somebody you've never met before, then that can make it very difficult to start meeting new positive people because you're not sure about the correct way to go about socializing and meeting somebody you've never spoken to.

Another thing that can hold you back is if you're a procrastinator, because as a procrastinator you might like the idea of becoming more positive, you might like the idea of going out there and meeting new people and talking to them or taking a new step to only think positive thoughts, but if you're someone that tends to put off taking that action it can hold you back.

If either of these two things is preventing you from moving forward, you're in luck. One, if you're struggling with procrastination, we have a very specific program that has been proven to change a person's habits completely. Our program makes a person completely destroy the procrastination they're suffering from, and they will find it easier to take action. In fact, this program is so easy and so proven to help people that we've drastically reduced the price so you can get it for less than what most people pay for a Starbucks. Even better, this program works so well that if it doesn't work for you, you can get your money back, because it's completely guaranteed.

The best thing about it is that it teaches you to make a few subtle tweaks to your everyday behavior, and suddenly procrastination completely vanishes. In fact, you can still be lazy, and defeat procrastination if you use the techniques that I'm going to share with you.

If you want to learn more about that procrastination program, go here: PsychologyHacker.com/Procrastination

Chapter 8: Improve the Quality of People in Your Life

There's an incredible quote I found on the internet, and despite a hell of a lot of research, I couldn't find who was the originator of it. But, it does ring true especially as it relates to this chapter. The phrase is this. "You cannot change the people around you, but you can change the people that you choose to be around." This is incredibly important because so many people love to blame their environment or blame the people around them, for holding them back. But the reality is, it is within your control to change the people who you choose to interact with.

I'll continue to talk about adding different people to your life, without losing the friends, connections and the network that you've already built yourself, throughout the rest of your life. Your social life is arguably one of the most important factors when it comes to determining your happiness. If people around you are incredibly sad, always depressed, and feeling bad you're going to spend a lot of your energy trying to build them up and that's energy you're spending on them, instead of spending on yourself. This also applies to your work and your career. If you're constantly at work helping everybody else with their projects and not completing your own tasks, the chance of you getting a pay raise or a promotion is significantly reduced. Conversely, if you're running your own business, and spending your time helping other people with their business, then your business isn't going to grow.

We can relate this to every single aspect of your life, from work to friendships, and even to your dating and intimate relationships. It's important that you develop and improve the quality of the people in your life if they're not helping you get to exactly where you want to be. Whether it's access to information for your work life, access to having fun in your friend life, or access to dating the kind of people you want in your relationship life, your happiness is 100% dependent on how you build up your connections, your network of people and the people you choose to socialize with.

Most people pick their social life based on two very simple factors: location and the proximity of the people that they interact with. What that means is, unless you've specifically gone out and attempted to grow your social life or improved the quality of people you typically spend time with, then all the people you hang out with are going to be the people who live near you, work near you, or randomly happen to be in the same place as you. If you're not hanging around in the kind of places that you want to be and are not interacting with the kind of people that you want to be around, then, you're not ever going to change your situation. You're always going to be stuck exactly where you are.

There are some common reasons why people never even attempt to improve their social life. One of the biggest is the fact that they like hanging out with the people they hang around with. You know, it's enjoyable to play video games with the same people that you've played video games with when you were a child. It's fun to go to work with the colleagues that you currently see every single day rather than, trying to network with people who are significantly higher up the ladder than you. Another reason people don't attempt to change their social life is they have social anxiety: fear of meeting other people. If the idea of interacting with strangers makes you feel uncomfortable, then it's a lot easier to spend time hanging out with the people that you already know.

Another big reason people don't change is the fact they dislike change. The idea of moving into a situation that's a little bit different, makes them feel awkward. They like things to be exactly where they are, that everything has its place. There's a set routine, and so, they don't want that to change. Therefore, they resist the idea of hanging out with new people. Finally, one of the biggest factors is they don't want to hang out with people they think are "snobbish." These people think they're better than everyone else. They think they've got a fancy car to prove how great they are. If you have a fear of interacting with people who are more successful than you, or you think those kinds of people might look down on you, then that can be a really big reason why you wouldn't make the change.

However, for every single one of these reasons, there's a counterpoint that explains why you probably should be doing it. I'm not saying you shouldn't hang out with the friends you grew up with; you definitely should. There should be an amount of time allocated to being with those friends. But, if they are the only people you interact with, then you are only going to have the exact same relation to them that you've always had. If they suddenly become incredibly successful, they're always going to look down on you because, they've known you since they were a kid and as far as they're concerned, you are the exact same person you were when you were younger. If they're pushing themselves to get better, there is a chance that you could rise up with them. But also, that can change the dynamic of the friendship.

The fun is in the fact that you sit around and play video games together or you go out to the same bars. The minute you change that, the minute you make it a business relationship, where you try and build something up together, then suddenly that original element is lost. It makes much more sense to develop an additional social circle where you can focus on improving yourself while still maintaining the original friendships and remembering what it's like to go back down to Earth.

Some of the most fun I have is when I interact with people who I knew when I was a kid, and they make fun of me. They don't dare treat me like I'm anything special because they only see me as I was back then and that's incredibly humbling. Sometimes it's really nice to get that sense of nostalgia when you're hanging out with your friends and not feeling particularly special. ON the other hand, other social circles have helped me to rise up. I see the people who look up to me and follow everything I do and everything I say. There's a lot of pressure to perform in those situations. I don't get to relax and completely be myself. Instead, I get to be somebody who forces them to push themselves to be even better.

Finally, I've got another social circle, who are all better than me. They all drive nicer cars than me. They all make more money than me. These guys are incredibly successful, to the tune of hundreds of millions of dollars. I like hanging around with them because they're the people that I get to learn from. By having these multiple social circles, I'm not just stuck in the same one that I grew up with, and it enables me to be a much richer and broader person.

For people who have social anxiety, you're always going to have social anxiety unless you do something to break it. One of the cool things about going out there and starting to break down that social anxiety is it enables you to network, and that helps you meet more people. There are lots of different ways to break down social anxiety. And in fact, we can devote and have devoted, entire videos in the past to getting over a fear of talking to strangers. You can slowly expose yourself to talking to strangers. Start off simply making friends with co-workers or people in your local coffee shop and then, move on from there.

For people who dislike change, you've got to remember that if you don't like change, then you're never going to get any. If you want your life to change and be different, then you need to start embracing that change. You need to look at change not as a bad thing, but as a good thing. Because, whether you like it, or not, change is going on all around you. I remember growing up and seeing the ideas of what the future might be like in the form of jetpacks and video TV conferencing. Now, they're so commonplace you can see them almost everywhere. Change happens. The more you embrace it, the more likely you are to be successful and to get the change that you want for your life.

When we think of snobbish people, often we feel this way because we're jealous that they've got something we haven't got. It's very rare that somebody who's successful decides to buy a fancy car so they can make everyone else feel bad. Most of the time, they buy it because they can. Sometimes they justify it because the quality is nicer. Or sometimes, it's a reward they promised themselves they'd get once they became successful. If you look down on people who do that, then you're going to hold yourself back because you're not going to want to "be one of them." By "be one of them," I mean, be successful. Be somebody who is capable of getting the nice things in their life. Think about what you can do to work hard to get to that position and remind yourself that it's still important to hang out with the people who aren't successful so that you can help them.

An incredibly important point to remember is that you should never confuse the people who are always around you, with the people who are there for you when you need them. A common mistake people make is, to think that. "Well, these friends have been there for me my entire life." When the reality is, they've probably *been around* you your entire life. That doesn't necessarily mean they've supported you in every single aspect. Maybe you've brought up something that you want to achieve, something you want to do, and your friends have held you back or made you feel bad about it. Or maybe, they've picked on you a bit for doing it. If that is the case, then those friends weren't really there for you. They were just around. They were just there. So, make sure you actually understand who these people are. I'm not saying you should cut ties with people who were there when you were younger. As I stated earlier, it's great to remind yourself of what it's like to hang with those people and to let loose a bit and be yourself. However, if you really want success, then you need to find the kind of people who are going to be there for you and who, you can be there for.

To recap, step one to improving the quality of people around you, is to section your social life. By combining all your friends into one big social circle, you run a huge risk of creating conflict between the different types of friends. For example, I love playing a lot of nerdy games like *Magic: The Gathering*, and *Dungeons and Dragons*, and I enjoy my fun social circle. But, I also like attending incredibly large masterminds with successful people who earn millions of dollars. If I tried to combine these two friend groups, there'd be a ton of arguments between them. The successful people would think it was a waste of time sitting around playing games because they've got their businesses to run. And the guys who like playing games will think they're enjoying life and that the people focusing on their business are not having fun every single day. These are two completely different social circles. I need both. I need to have fun but, I also need to focus on my business and grow it. So, I keep the social circles separate.

The other problem with creating conflict between different friends as you try and merge everything together is that if the more successful ones think that drama and arguments are a waste of time, they are going to distance themselves from the group and ultimately, from you. They're not going to want to be around you. They're not going to want to spend their time with you. Meaning, you're going to miss out on another aspect that could have been kept completely separate, in its own, unique social circle. Separate social circles enable you to enjoy different activities with different people. You don't have to try and force your friends who like playing video games to go hiking with you and climb up a giant mountain.

By making sure that each of your interests has a different social circle, you've got many different groups of people you can socialize with. You've got a much richer social life. More importantly, the final part of this step is to remember that if one of the social circles breaks down, you won't lose all your friends. Say, for example, the dating social circle, which contains all the girls you like socializing with, going out and partying with and of course, picking the girls to date from goes terribly wrong, you won't lose your friend groups. You don't have to worry about the backlash of a girlfriend who you go partying with, suddenly affecting your business because they've stayed separate. Because you've never merged them, you don't have to worry about something falling apart. If you get into a falling out over a board game, you don't have to worry about that affecting your dating life.

Keep these different social circles separate. I have the people who I work with, and I have the people who I play games with. I have the people who I try and grow my business with, in terms of my mentors and similar types of relationships. Then, I have the people I grew up with. The people who know me exactly as I am. By having these four distinct social circles, not to mention my family social circle, I've made sure my life is compartmentalized, and they only cross when they absolutely must. I'm talking about big group events like birthdays. But typically, I try and keep each of these groups separate. On events like my birthday, I'll often arrange multiple events. I'll have a birthday party with the friendlier ones, and then, I'll have a business dinner with the people who I want to focus on improving my standing or connection with.

Step two is to add value. Every single group has a leech. You call them the "freeloader" and you know they never pay for a round of drinks. They never have anything cool to add. They insult people, and they carry on with the group because they've got nothing better to do. That's fine; every group is going to have one. Don't let it be you. A friend of mine used to say, "If you're wondering who the leech is in the group and you can't identify them, then there's a good chance it is you." The point is, you need to be the person who adds value to everybody, whichever group you're in. If you're in a board game group, then you need to be the one suggesting which board games to play, and you need to come up with good board games for everybody to enjoy. Maybe you're even the one who provides the board games or, stays up to date with the latest releases.

On the other hand, if you're part of the business group, then you want to be the one who adds the most value. Make sure you're learning as much as you can, reading as many books as possible, suggesting different books for people to read. If it's a nightclub group, then you want to be the first one to buy the rounds. You don't have to buy every round. But make sure you buy the first round, because that's the one everybody is going to remember.

By making sure you add value to the group, the group is going to see value in you, and they're going to want to make sure that you stay around. That's going to keep you in the upper echelons in the group hierarchy. That's going to make everybody want to include you, and so they will invite you to everything they do.

Now, a very good way to add value to a group is to do it on an individual basis. Don't think about adding value to the whole group. Think about adding value to each individual person. A phrase I often say when I first start coaching somebody is: "What's the biggest thing you're trying to achieve right now?" Or, "What's your biggest struggle?" Or, "What's the pain point that you're trying to resolve right now?" Any version of these kinds of questions related to a specific point is a smart way of finding out what somebody else is trying to achieve. Once you do that, then you can keep an ear out to solve their problem if you can't solve it straight away. Whenever I meet somebody within a business social circle, I'll almost always say to them. "What's the biggest pain point in your business? What are you trying to resolve?" If they say anything that I've heard a solution to or I know a book that solves it, I'll say. "Have you read this book?" or "Do you know this guy?" If they say, "No." I say, "I think it/they might have the solution you're looking for." It'll make an instant connection. They see that I'm valuable. They see that I'm knowledgeable, and it'll cement my position in the group.

On the other hand, when it comes to friends, I might say to somebody. "Hey, what are you trying to work toward right now? What are you trying to achieve?" Then I'll listen to whatever is going on in their life. Sometimes, they'll have a dating problem which I have no problem solving. But sometimes the problem will be around a board game they're trying to buy or something they're trying to build, or maybe they're trying to create their own game. Once again, I can keep an ear out and see if I've got any great suggestions I can give to them.

Step three is probably the most important part of increasing the quality of people in your life. Everything I've spoken about is incredibly important. It revolves around the tactics and the strategy of making sure you're adding value, so people want you to be in their life. Assuming you've compartmentalized your social groups, you're not worried about blurring them all together; you don't have to worry about any negative impact happening. More importantly, it enables you to have multiple groups so you can have higher and higher quality of friends in other groups without losing the friends you already have. But, this is the key element.

Are you somebody who is 100% convicted when you speak to somebody that you mean what you say? I sat up late one night watching a TV show, and a religious program came on. I'm not particularly religious but there was something that was said inside the particular sermon that had me watching at three o'clock in the morning, and that struck true with me. I realized what I was watching wasn't about religion. It was something that every single human being should be doing on the planet. It occurred to me that I need to apply this saying to my life and the minute that I added it to the way I spoke to people, everything in my life changed. The way that people responded to me was different. The way that people wanted to interact with me changed. This one phrase enabled me to make friends, instantly.

You can hang out with rich people at a mastermind, a business networking event or you can go to a brand-new board game night and meet new friends. Or you can go out to the highest, hottest nightclub in the world. But, when you speak to any of these people, adding value means they need to believe what you're saying is real. You need to sound sincere. You need to 100% have the intent behind the words that you mean what you say. The phrase that I saw on television that completely blew my mind was this: "When you say, 'thank you,' do you really give thanks?"

We say "thank you" every single day. You say "thank you" to somebody who hands you a coffee in the coffee shop. You say "thank you" to somebody in Whole Foods as you do your grocery shopping. You say "thank you" multiple times every single day. But, every time you say, "thank you," have you given thanks or said an automatic reply?

You're not a robot; you're a human being. You're supposed to say "thank you" with conviction. It's supposed to mean something. Along that same line, when you give a compliment, do you mean it? Or are you trying to get a person to like you? Because there's a big difference between these two intentions. I can safely say that every single time I've given somebody a compliment, I've meant it. I'm going to share with you an example of the difference between saying "thank you" and giving thanks. When I am talking to somebody in a checkout line or when I'm in the bank, for instance, I make sure I always give thanks, and this is how people remember you. There's no magic, no special tricky words. No, this is the mind-blowing technique that makes people do whatever you want. It's a way of saying "thank you" that is genuine and sincere. It's something that every single person should do.

If somebody handed me my coffee, I used to say, "Thank you." Likely "Thanks," as most people say. I'm saying the word. I'm doing it as a matter of protocol, but I don't truly mean it. Now, when somebody hands me my coffee, I always respond like this: "Thank you ever so much. Really appreciate it." I'm adding intent to what I'm saying. I'm staring into their eyes; I'm focusing. I mean what I say, and they know it in that moment of me saying, "Thank you ever so much. I really appreciate it." Doing this makes a real connection. They'll often look up and lock eye contact with me, and then I'll say to them, with complete intention. "Really, have a good day today." Not just, "Have a nice day." "Really, have a good day. I hope they don't work you too hard." If you've hung out with me long enough, you'll notice that this is how I talk to people. This is what makes the real connections. It's what makes me stand out.

The funny thing is, it's not necessarily about conducting yourself in this way to people in your social circle. It's about people in my social circle, seeing me treat others this way. When I treat a waiter or a waitress with intent, with compassion, with giving thanks, I am proving that I am a decent person. That I care about people. That I'm a people person and that is what makes social groups want you to be around. The point of a social group is to be social. It's to have groups of people interact. If they see excellence, if they see somebody capable of interacting socially with excellence, they want you to stay around. They want you to be part of it.

This goes even further if you're actually interacting with a group. Because sometimes when you ask somebody,

"What's the problem?" Or, "What are you trying to solve?" They're going to tell you a story or share their point of view. It's really easy at this point to blank out and start thinking of an answer or another question. Instead, there's a much better exercise that can help develop empathy which is what makes real connections with people. It triggers oxytocin in their mind, which as you know if you've watched my videos, is going to form a very strong bond between you and other people.

If you want to learn how Oxytocin affects your brain, visit:

PsychologyHacker.com/Oxytocin

Imagining yourself in their situation and asking yourself, *what would I do if that happened to me*? Is going to enable you to be present in the situation. This will help you to truly connect with people and hopefully, trigger some of the feelings of what they're going through, so you can sympathize with them, empathize with them and more importantly, come up with solutions of what you would do in their shoes. The next time somebody says to you, "I'm really worried I might lose my job." Don't respond, with

"Oh wow, that sucks." Think, *what would I do if I was losing my job? How would I feel? How have I felt in the past when I've gone through that?* Take a moment and imagine yourself in their shoes. If they say, "You've gone quiet, are you okay?" Reply, "You know what? I was imagining what it would be like to go through what you're going through, and I was remembering the time I lost my job before and how devastating it feels. This is really tough. I'm so sorry about what you're going through."

Then, take a moment and try and solve their problem. This is where the adding value comes in. This is where you can say. "I know some people who work in your industry, maybe one of them has got an opening. I'd be more than happy to ask. Even though, I know you haven't lost your job yet. Might be good to have something else lined up. And who knows, it might even pay more." That's what it means to add value. That's what it means to be authentically connected and to speak with intention. That's what it takes to improve the quality of the people in your life. When you're this excellent at communicating, it doesn't matter if the person you're talking to drives an expensive Maserati or a Lamborghini. It doesn't matter if they're a CEO of a joint fortune 500 company because you're excellent at something else. Something important. You're excellent at communicating and at being human. At socializing. People who are successful will appreciate that.

You know who else appreciates that? Everyone else. Every friend you grew up with. Every friend you meet in a social circle. Every friend you interact with. Everybody you meet at work. Every single person cares about communication. And when you apply these methods, you are being excellent at being yourself. By being present. Speaking with intent and caring about what you're saying, is what it takes to build up your social circle.

I want you to remember one last important insight.

Sometimes when you're trying to improve yourself, trying to reach different goals, the people around you won't understand what you're doing. I don't want you to worry about that because it's not for them; it's for you.

Next Steps: If you are looking for like-minded people, the ones dedicated to adding value and building each other up, I'd recommend checking out my exclusive Facebook Group, Psych Hackers. It's composed of current and former students of mine, many of whom have massively improved their lives over the past few years. They're always looking for ambitious new people to meet, and they've got a ton of great experiences that they're more than willing to share. Use this link to join the group and start meeting new people who want the exact same thing you do: PsychologyHacker.com/Group

Chapter 9: The Active Listening Blueprint

A number of key psychological hacks you can apply to your brain have a dramatic, incredible effect on your life, for the better.

But the one hack you'd really want to put into play is active listening. In fact, Stanford Business School conducted a study in 2013, where they analyzed different CEOs to find what the CEOs felt they should learn the most or improve the most.

Active listening scored as one of the highest things that most CEOs wished they were better at practicing. The problem with this is you can't Google the answer. If you Google "active listening," you're going to get pretty lame advice. You'll read: "Make sure you're focusing on the other person," or, "Keep your shoulders aimed at them," or, "Try cocking your head to one side while you're listening."

You might even read: "Repeat back to the person what they just said to you." Believe it or not, none of these are going to get across the fact that you're actively listening, and they're not likely to help you actively listen in the first place. When it comes down to active listening, there are two elements.

The reason you want to actively listen is that one, you want to be better at listening. You want to make sure you're actually hearing and understanding what the other person is saying. On the flip side, the other person has to know that you are actively listening to what they say. If either one of these elements is missing, then you're really not actively listening. That's the problem with most of the generic advice you find about active listening on the internet.

I took part in a class a long time ago. It was part of an NLP initiative, and the teacher was teaching us through active listening. The advice given was to place your tongue on the roof of your mouth, open up your palms toward the person you're talking to, and then sit there and nod every time they said something important.

At the end of it, once they'd finished talking to you, you were to repeat back to them exactly what they'd said, to show you understood it. The truth is, I was capable of doing that, and passively listening. I could put my hands in those positions, move my tongue to the roof of my mouth, and then I could still sit there and think about the game, or the weekend, or whatever else it was that I was going to do that day.

When I tried this technique in the real world and repeated back to the person what was said, one of two things happened. Either A) They felt that I was actively listening, even though I wasn't, or B) I'd repeat back to them, and they'd recognize what I was doing as some kind of active listening technique I'd read on the internet. It made them doubt whether I had truly listened to exactly what was said.

At our studio where we help people improve their business, and life, by teaching them real psychological hacks to dramatically change their life for the better, we teach a very specific technique for active listening. We focus on the most important word of "active listening," which is the active part.

The listening part is something you're capable of doing, but it can be passive listening. It could be active listening. Of all the types of listening, the active part is what differentiates active listening from any other kind of listening. The reason that someone shares something with you is that they want to. They want to experience it with you, or more importantly, they want you to experience it with them.

When you need to practice active listening, you need to do what is called "actioning." This is the best psychological hack I can give you for active listening, to action what you're hearing as often as possible. Don't just make a note of it. Don't repeat what you've heard back to the person who said it. Action it. In other words, *take action* on it. Whatever the other person is saying to you, actually go out there and do the action as fast as possible.

This is going to have a huge impact not only on your active listening skills but on the way other people treat you when they realize that you are an incredible active listener. First of all, if you know for a fact that you're going to have to action whatever is being said to you, you're going to pay attention, because you're not going to want to get it wrong.

That would make it look like you hadn't listened to a thing they'd said, so it *makes* you need to actively listen. You have to be sure everything they've said is 100%, so you know that what you're going to put into action is going to be correct.

Secondly, and arguably more importantly, when you put into action something as fast as possible, you're teaching others you're somebody who not only actively listens, but you take action as well. After a short period, the people around you will note that you are an action taker; they will see the active part of active listening, coming into effect.

People are going to trust you more often. Doing this will show them you're the kind of person they can trust to actually get things done. If they want to hire somebody for their business, or if they want to give you more business, they're much more likely to pick somebody who is an active listener, and an action taker.

I am known throughout the world to business and psychological circles, for internet marketing. In all the different social circles I'm part of, I am somebody who's a speed implementer. What that means is as soon as I finish a conversation with somebody, I'll often take the first couple of steps to get what we talked about done, whether it's hiring the right team, or setting a date to have a brainstorming session. Whatever it is, I take the simplest, easiest, first step to actively take action on what I've heard from other people.

This makes people feel very comfortable giving me tasks or telling me things they want to happen, and it puts me in the wonderful position where I get to choose whether I'm going to take action or not. While actively listening, I can say, "This isn't something that I'm going to do," and it gives me that position of being someone who gets to say no, or more importantly, gives me the chance to say yes when there's something I really want to do.

When you are in that position of being somebody who can say yes or no, and when people trust and know you're the kind of person who's going to do what you need to, it means you've got a wealth of people giving you opportunities and chances to succeed. You get to pick and choose the ones you want. When I do this, it gives me a much more powerful position when it comes to negotiating. It gives me a better position when it comes to my social life.

Active listening has become a powerful toolset in my own arsenal. This little psychological hack takes you from thinking, *I'm going to really focus on hearing what they say*, to, *if I'm going to action everything they're saying, what do I have to get done?*

The irony behind this is sometimes when I'm actively listening; it doesn't even look like I'm listening to the other person, because I might be so eager to get something actioned that in the middle of their explanation, I'll ask them questions about it, which looks like I'm interrupting. It looks like I'm not even really focused on what they're saying, at least to somebody on the outside.

But the person I'm talking to gets blown away because they realize I'm engaging them. I'm deeply talking to them about their subject and understanding exactly what they're saying. They know we're connected, and I've given them my full attention. Not only that, I'm giving them my cognitive power that I use to think to help them solve, establish or achieve whatever it is that they want to achieve.

That is the true power of active listening, being somebody who gets things done, being known as an action taker. But, one thing will completely destroy your chance at being a good active listener. That is a lack of confidence. If you don't feel confident, if you don't feel like you are a person who could get things done, or you don't feel like you're going to do the right thing, that lack of confidence can completely destroy all your intentions to try and help somebody.

If you say to yourself, *I really like the idea of helping somebody, but what if I'm too tired tomorrow? What if I've got too much work? What if I do it wrong?* All those thoughts can completely destroy your ability to actively listen, and they can hold you back. That's why one of the next most important psychological hacks that I tell everyone they should focus on learning, is learning how to hack your own confidence.

Next Steps: To better understand how to develop an actionable active-listening plan, use this link to see a quick video detailing how you can take immediate action and avoid procrastinating when it comes to working with others: PsychologyHacker.com/Action

Chapter 10: Developing Killer Confidence

If I went out into the street and asked people "If you could flick a switch and hack into your own psychology and completely change it, what is the one thing that you wish would happen the fastest inside your own brain?" I would argue that probably eight out of 10 people would say that the thing they wish they could change would be their confidence level.

What's funny is, if I took some of those people who believed that they're confident and I got them in a private room where nobody was around, and nobody was going to judge them, and I asked them how confident they felt on a day to day basis, I would probably find that even the few who said they don't have a problem with confidence actually deep down are still struggling with confidence.

Confidence is one of those things that tends to be the solution everybody gives you to everything. If you're struggling to get a new job, everyone's like "Don't worry about it." "Don't worry about it," really means "Be more confident." Or if you're trying to attract somebody, they're like, "Oh, just be yourself." What they mean is not to worry about it. In fact, the average piece of dating advice that somebody's going to give you to improve your dating life is to be confident, and you'll be fine.

Most of the time, confidence is attributed to the success of the average person. Somebody who is successful is seen as confident, and somebody who is confident is seen as successful. That's why this next psychological hack is all about how to help you become more confident. In fact, it's one of the first things that we teach people when they come here to work with us privately. Whether we're helping somebody grow their business, whether we're helping somebody improve their dating life or whether we're helping somebody build a better social circle, whatever it comes down to, we start with teaching people the key to confidence. And miraculously, confidence is something that you can develop.

Where people tend to go wrong, however, is they think of confidence as an all-encompassing thing, that once you have confidence, you are now confident. Where the reality is, you tend to be confident in certain areas. For example, you might be confident at Christmas time around your parents, sitting down having dinner. Or you might be confident sitting with your family, teaching them something that you've learned at work during the day. But you might not be confident when it comes to talking to a stranger in a bar or going to a networking meeting, or the one that everybody tends to struggle with, standing on stage and talking to people. Public speaking is one of the biggest fears most people admit to feeling unconfident about.

The truth is, confidence comes from one thing. If you want a psychological hack to completely change the way you feel, to make you feel more confident, this is the hack that you need to understand, because the core of it is teaching you that confidence comes from experience. If you want to become more confident, the key isn't to think, *how do I become more confident overall*? It's to think, *how do I become confident in a specific area*? Once you become confident in that area, you can move onto another area. You might want to become more confident at the gym, in which case you can apply the technique that I'm about to teach you that can help you build more experience rapidly—and that translates into confidence. So, you'll feel more confident at the gym, and then you can move that confidence to become more confident in the workplace, or more confident in interviews or more confident standing onstage and publicly speaking.

When you break it down into different areas, what happens is, over time, you become confident overall. You're not actually confident holistically; you're confident in more areas. Most people tend to stick to the areas where they already feel confident. For example, somebody might be confident online when they're playing a video game. They might be confident in the workplace and might be confident when they order Starbucks or spend time with their family. However, outside of those areas, they tend to be shy, a little bit reclusive and they would probably describe themselves as an introvert. However, if they spent a little more time trying to become more confident at a local bar, out at a networking event for their work and also practicing on public speaking, they would find their confidence would transition to other areas. They would feel more confident in a big group speaking in a bar. They'd feel more confident when they're out and about with people they don't really know as they realize that everybody feels unconfident, and people tend to look up to the people who are more confident.

A psychological experiment was done by Stanley Milgram on obedience that found that confidence and authority tend to be the quality we look up to when we follow people. If people are looking for a leader or looking for someone to take charge, they're going to look for the person who has the most authority, or confidence, about a specific situation. Learning how to hack your psychology to be more confident in a specific area is a great way to help yourself succeed at anything, whether it's in your workplace when you're trying to get a new job, in your business, or in sales. In any area, you need to learn how to hack your own confidence, and as I said earlier, you do that through experience.

When we're talking about hacking confidence, we're really talking about hacking experience, and the key is for you to become as experienced in a subject as quickly as possible so that experience can translate into confidence. Let's break this down into two sections. The first hack concerns how you can get the theoretical experience before you go out there and do it, and then, how to get the practical experience that translates into real confidence. The theoretical experience is easy.

First, go online, or to your favorite bookstore, and order three of the highest rated books on the subject where you want to improve. I would look for books that have four and a half or five-star reviews and have hundreds of people reviewing it, saying it's a great book. I'd find one that was aimed at beginners like a getting started, how-to, or a guide for dummies, and then I'd look at two that were more expert. When I got my hands on them, I'd read them in order. So, read the beginner one first. By the time I'd finished three books, which would probably take me a week or two if I was focusing on getting it done, and still concentrating on having a life and doing everything else that I wanted to do, that experience would have given me a lot of knowledge.

I've learned, once I know the jargon, I'm capable of having key conversations with experts in the industry. At that point, I usually hire somebody to guide me through the process. In these scenarios, I'm looking for a mentor. I'm looking for somebody who has experience in a particular field, and I'm looking to pay them, usually a premium rate for their time, so that I can ask them a very specific set of questions.

Next, you'd reach out to a service like the one we offer where we have consultants that you can talk to; or who you can ask questions about the correct steps to grow your business. You can ask about earning more money, improving your dating life, building your social life, or if you wanted to become an ace in tennis, then you'd try to find a specific coach to help you with tennis. You will hire these people ideally at their maximum rate. You don't want to negotiate because you want them to feel good about working with you and for them to give you value. If you manage to get a half-rate deal, then realistically, the person will only put in half the amount of effort. They don't feel that they want to help you entirely. When you pay above and beyond, you'll find that people genuinely want to help you become successful.

When I've struggled for money in the past, and I've needed to hire an expert, I'd work out what their hourly rate was, and then I'd hire them for say four hours but tell them I only wanted two hours' worth of work. Even though I couldn't afford 10 hours or so, by telling them that I'm willing to pay double for less time, it makes them feel like they want to help me because I'm technically paying twice as much as anyone else even though it's only for two hours of work.

I tend to find that people will often then gift me additional hours because they feel guilty that I'm not taking as much of their time as I'm supposed to. I typically get a much better deal even though initially I was willing to pay twice as much. Once you use this technique, you get to talk to an absolute expert. Somebody who's devoted, who has spent five, ten, fifteen years, becoming an expert on a very specific subject. Once you've got them, you're going to ask them specific questions. Tell them the books you've read. Tell them what you want to achieve, and then ask them to give you a breakdown of the different steps you need to get there. Do they have any other books they can recommend that can guide you through the process? How often do they recommend you should put time into getting this done? And what should you focus on next?

Once you've taken those steps, you don't need to talk to them that much more. If you've got any time left over, I would suggest that you touch base with them a month later to follow up on what the next steps will be. You now know what you need to work on, and that's when we move onto the practical aspect. Because the real key to getting experience; the real key to confidence comes from failure. You don't learn anything by being successful. If you go out there and try something and you succeed, then all you've learned is that whatever you did worked, but you don't know what might have gone wrong. You don't know how to fix something that goes wrong. Real confidence comes from knowing that if a plan goes wrong, you have the knowledge to handle it.

You might be an amazing driver, but the best drivers are the ones who know if something goes wrong, they can handle it. They know what to do if they hit ice on the road. They know what to do if one of their tires blows. They know what to do if somebody tries to cut them off in traffic. The key is knowing what to do when what you're trying out goes wrong. The only way you will know that is through the experience of things going wrong. The reason I tend to get very good and very confident very fast is that I actively seek out failure. Even if I find a process that's successful, I'll stop doing what's successful and test a bunch of different ways to see if those other ways fail. One of two things happen. I either find another way to be successful or more than likely; I learn how to recover from failure.

By being somebody who seeks out the most failure, I learn how to recover from the most failures, and this creates a lot of confidence in a subject. Even if I'm not an absolute expert in it, I become an expert in the failure of it, which actually helps me teach beginners better. It helps me understand the process, plan or action better, and more importantly, it helps me to be more confident. Even if I'm dealing with somebody who "has more actual time studying," they may not be as experienced at failing as I am, and that helps me succeed at far greater levels.

But of course, you can completely crush your ability to do this, and that will happen if you take a risk that is too far for you to reach to. If you seek out failure and you wind up in a position where you can't possibly recover from that failure, a failure that maybe is life-threatening or dangerous or financially crippling, then, of course, that whole experience wasn't worthwhile, and you can no longer move forward. That's why one of the other psychological hacks that I think you really want to focus on, is learning how to choose the right risks.

Learning what risks you should be taking and when to take them is one of the keys to ensuring your experience at becoming confident is going to have the best effect for you.

You can go to this link for more help on learning about taking risks: PsychologyHacker.com/Risks

Chapter 11: First Steps to Making More Money

Let's talk about the first steps to making more money. This works whether you're working a basic 9:00 to 5:00, or if you run your own $1 million business. There's a great quote by Warren Buffet that says, "Today, people who hold cash equivalents feel comfortable. They shouldn't. They have opted for a terrible long-term asset, one that pays virtually nothing and is certain to depreciate in value." What I love about this quote is it talks about the fact that cash doesn't increase over time. It decreases. If you think you've got a great job that pays you well and you've got solid savings in your bank account, you are not safe; you are not secure, and your value will depreciate over time.

It doesn't matter whether you're in a highly paid job or if you're in a lower paid job or even if you run your own business. The key and the steps you need to take to make more money and to experience growth involve getting the right kind of mindset. If you practice what I am about to share with you, you'll move into a different position where you're earning more money. I've practiced this mindset hack numerous times in the past.

I grew up in east London. I'm a true-blue cockney. And I grew up in an area of London that's known for being particularly violent, full of crime, and more importantly, we had literally no money. I was raised by my stepdad and my mother. My stepdad was a truck driver. My mother was a stay-at-home mom, and she used to work when she was younger as a stripper. That's how we got by. We had very little money. It was my sister and me. I remember food like bacon was always fought over in the household because it was a luxury we couldn't afford.

There is a saying I heard growing up in East London: "You'll never get out of East London." The idea being that the only jobs that would be available to an East Londoner because of their accent are never going to be that good. I managed to break out. I managed to change my life. I have everything I could ever possibly have dreamt of as a kid, and yet I still remember the mindset we're discussing. I still take the steps every single day to make more money. Because the money that I already have isn't good enough.

It's a depreciating asset. I'm constantly pushing myself to go further.

This is the method I use to keep that mindset; it's how I go about making sure I'm constantly improving and pushing myself to reach the next level. There's another great quote by Warren Buffet: "The best investment you can make is in yourself." If you want to make more money, then you need to set aside time to make more money.

A lot of people wish they made more money, but they won't necessarily make it unless there is an amount of time set aside specifically to help them grow money and to help them make more money. Whether you're in a 9:00 to 5:00, or if you run a business, there's a good chance that at some point you've plateaued, and making money is about breaking through that barrier and moving into the next level.

It would be very easy for me to settle and say, "I've got a nice house. I've got a nice car. I can relax and just enjoy." But the reality is, if I do that then it's only a matter of time before something goes wrong and it all disappears. I'm constantly pushing. Constantly trying to achieve more. It's hard because we often think of money as the key to being comfortable. We might say, "Life's tough. Life's hard right now. If I had more money, everything would be okay. I'd be comfortable." But if you want more, then you constantly have to force yourself to be uncomfortable again. Once you get into that comfortable state, it's easy to stay there for a few years. But the reality is, if you want your life to continue to stay comfortable, then you have to force yourself to be uncomfortable, where you're constantly pushing to get more money rather than waiting for everything to fall apart and then scrambling.

You can think of it like the carrot and the stick. The donkey can either walk toward the carrot, or it can run away from the stick. Well, it's a much more pleasant experience if it's constantly chasing the carrot rather than waiting for the stick to hit its ass every single time. That's how you want to view money. It sucks that money is such a big part of our lives, but the reality is, it is what makes the world go 'round. It is what helps us move and achieve things. That's why we have to put aside a certain part of our time every week, and every day toward making money and, of course, toward growing it into making more.

People make common mistakes when they're trying to increase their money. I see these errors all the time from students of mine or even from friends. One of the first is they wait for a pay rise. I remember when I was a kid I used to think that if I earned $1,000 per year for every year that I was alive, then that would be a good fee. When I was 19 years old, I said, "If I earned 19,000 pounds, that would be good enough." When I was 21, it was: "If I make 21,000 pounds, that's great." The logic follows then that I thought, *when I'm 45, I should earn 45,000 pounds.* In my head, that was a good amount of money to earn.

In contrast, last week I made $36,000. I made $36,000 in a single week last week. I'm 35 years old, so according to my 19-year-old self, that should have been a year's salary. The reason that that changed for me is that I wasn't waiting to get a pay rise. I wasn't waiting for my boss to give me more money. I wasn't hoping he would give me a portion of what he made. Instead, I went out there with the intention to make money. Don't wait for someone to give it to you. Create it.

Another big mistake that people make is they'll get inspired by something like this book, and they'll quit their job to start their own business. A great friend of mine was a talent scout. He made a lot of money. He cast a lot of feature films, by placing B-list actors in films, and then wanted to be a filmmaker. He had $25,000 saved when he decided it was enough money for him to live on for at least six months. The plan was to run his business for six months and then be successful.

For six months he lived off that $25,000 and his business didn't take off. It didn't get anywhere. So, at the end of the six months, he had to get a job. He couldn't get a job as a talent scout again because there's a lot of competition for those jobs. By the time he tried to get back his old job, it had already gone to somebody else. He ended up working at Apple in the Genius Bar as their tech support. His entire life changed because he quit his job and started his business.

Another reason that people don't make money is that they don't like selling. I can't tell you how many people I've met who have said, "I hate the idea of selling. I want somebody else to do that for me." A very good friend of mine, one of my business mentors said, "You want to be as close to the money as possible." The closest place you can be to the money is selling. If you're selling, you are literally taking the money in your hand. The closer you are to it, the better chance there is for you to make more money. Look at the *Wolf of Wall Street* and see how much money you can make in sales.

I don't care whether you're trying to get a better job, in which case you will be selling yourself, or whether you're starting your own business, in which case you're selling your services. It doesn't matter if you're a doctor or a chiropractor, it's exactly the same. You're still selling something. You're selling your service to people. You need to be an expert in sales. If you want to make money, then you've got to accept the fact that sales is something you must excel in. You should read books on sales. You should understand sales. You should practice sales and improve your skills.

The next objection is a big one. I often talk to people starting their business for the first time. And, of course, one very good way of making more money is to start a business. It's people who play at business rather than running it who don't succeed. When you're playing at business, you're putting a lot more energy into things like logos, business cards, websites, stationary that's got your name on it, and you're going around and talking to people about it. Whereas, when you're actually running a business, you often don't have time to build that stuff. I don't have a business card. My websites aren't always 100% functional. I don't have as big an online presence as we probably could have. But that's because we focus on running the business versus playing at business. We don't care so much about what the website looks like as long as we're hitting all our targets financially.

By putting our financial targets first, it's a lot easier to forget about the website for a while, but we'll handle those issues later. That's the correct way to do it. You want to focus on making the sales and money first. Which, of course, helps you live. Then, you can focus on all the other stuff like branding.

It is possible for you to earn more money within one month. But there's a lot of reasons why people don't do it. One of the main reasons is they value their free time more than making money. There are a lot of TV shows I have never seen. I haven't seen *Daredevil* on Netflix. I haven't seen *Damien,* which is the show that I really want to watch on Netflix. I've only just started watching *Walking Dead.* I still haven't finished watching *Breaking Bad.* I really don't have a good Netflix habit. The TV that I do watch is usually on date nights with my girlfriends so I can spend quality time sitting down with them and hugging them.

I also don't play many video games because I value earning and building my business a lot more than I value my free time. If I do have any free time, I tend to spend it on what I really care about, i.e., bonding with my friends, bonding with my family, or my partners. I make sure that I have healthy relationships, so the sacrifice is the leisure time that other people use to relax.

Another reason why people stop earning money is they've stopped learning. If you're not learning, then everybody else is moving ahead of you. Everyone else is improving. If you want to be the best at sales, then you need to learn the best methods. If you want to be the best at running a business, then you need to learn how to run your business the best. If you're selling education, then you need to be the most educated. If you're doing artwork, then you need to make sure you're learning about all the latest artistic methods. Whatever it is that you're doing, you need to learn about it constantly.

If you think back and remember that the last topic you learned about was a few years ago, then it's time to change it up and dedicate time to learning and improvement.

A friend of mine was a plastic surgeon. He spent years, and years, and years becoming a plastic surgeon. Then he finally became a plastic surgeon, got his own office and made okay money, but he had the mentality of *my boss is never going to give me a pay raise. I need to run my own plastic surgery office. In which case, I need to be experienced at running a business. I need to think about how to build up that business.* Then he realized that wasn't his skill set. Years, and years, and years he had dedicated to his pursuit. He was a skilled plastic surgeon, but terrible at business. So, he had to learn that process all over again.

It's never too late to start. If you're in school focusing on your education, at some point you're going to want to learn business. And you need to learn how to sell.

Another valid reason for why somebody doesn't want to earn more money is because they simply don't want to earn more money. If you've plateaued, if you are comfortable, if you are earning the right amount of money and your money's in investments and growing not depreciating, great. Don't worry about it. You don't have to do anything. But I'm going to argue that you do want to apply what I teach you. In particular, if you do want more money, then you really need to pay attention.

Remember this: if you are not growing, you are shrinking. That's because everybody else is growing. If you're not pushing yourself to be better, everybody else is. Technically, because they're getting bigger, you're getting smaller. You have to push yourself. You have to grow. Think about what you could be doing to make more money to grow yourself. It doesn't necessarily mean that you have to quit your day job.

Again, step one, you have to make time to make money. A lot of people don't have any time in their week to make more money. They spend it watching Netflix, or they spend it sitting down watching TV or browsing porn. But if you don't have time to set aside to actually make money, then you're not going to make more money. Part of every week should be devoted specifically to your bread and butter earnings.

As I told you, my stepdad was a truck driver. He'd say to me, "Most of the jobs I do each week are just to cover the bread and butter." What he meant by that is his jobs paid the bills. He knew how much he had to work on his truck driving trips, how many hours he had to put in to pay all of the bills. That included food. That included rent. That included gas, electric, water and every other expense we needed to pay to get by. Everything else he did on top of that was growth.

A great tactic to take if you're starting a new business or venture is to say, "My day job needs to cover the basics. It needs to cover all of my bills and everything else I need." If you can complete in a 9:00 to 5:00 day all the work you need to do for your day job, then you know that at the end of the month it pays all the basic bills. Maybe it doesn't give you anything left in your pocket. That's okay because now you know that any extra hours you put in after the 9:00 to 5:00 are all growth. This is the spending money, the money you can put into building a business. That's the way that you want to think about it. So, make sure that your bread and butter are covered. Once they're covered, it's time to think about growth.

A part of each week should be dedicated to learning how to make money doing what you love. If we assume you're in a 9:00 to 5:00 job, if you're going to put the next three hours at the end of every day, from 5:00 to 8:00 into building a business or making more money or to selling something, you should be selling something you love. You should be doing something you love. Because otherwise, you're putting your free time into an area you don't really care about. There's no point doing a 9:00 to 5:00 in a job that you don't care about, and then doing three hours working in a car wash. Sure, maybe it helps you make ends meet. But if you don't love it, if you're not passionate about washing cars, then maybe that isn't the right choice for you. If the 9:00 to 5:00 is making ends meet, then the 5:00 to 8:00, or the 5:00 to 9:00, or the 5:00 to 10:00, should be doing something else.

When I first started learning the dating world, I didn't have much money. I put all my savings into learning how to be good at dating. During the day, I was a janitor. My entire day, right up until I clocked out at 7:00 p.m. was all about being a janitor. I knew I wanted to make money in the evenings, and I knew I wanted to make money in a way that helped me meet girls. Some of my friends had become charity collectors. They'd go out in the street and collect money for charities, and then they would flirt with all the hot girls. I kind of liked the idea, but it didn't help me go to nightclubs.

To make it work for me, I worked until 7:00 p.m., and then I would sleep for a couple of hours. I would wake up at 9:00, eat and go to a nightclub at 10:00. From 10:00 until

3:00, I was partying in the nightclub. There, I would meet girls, and then I would invite them to other nightclubs, and I would get paid for bringing girls in because I was a promoter. The janitor job paid my bills, my food, my rent and my other living expenses. The money I got as a promoter was my bonus money. But the cool thing was I was getting paid to meet and attract women. I got paid directly based on my ability to sell girls on coming to the nightclubs.

I learned selling. I had a business I cared about. It was my free time. It was doing what I wanted to be doing anyway, which was going out and meeting girls. But I was also earning money from it. Eventually, I was capable of earning a month's salary in a single week of doing the promotion because you don't get paid much as a janitor. At a certain point, I was earning 2,000, 3,000, even one time up to 5,000 pounds for just one week of promoting, because I was bringing such a high volume of people to the clubs. Having that secondary system, and separating it gives you the chance to make more money. You'll love it because you'll be learning while you're working.

If you are going to build your own business, then you need to make sure that two or three days of that week aren't based on designing a website, aren't based on fulfilling tasks; a part of each week should be based specifically on selling and getting new customers.

Step two: Have something to sell. You can't have a business unless you've got something to sell, and a way to make money. It doesn't matter whether it's a product or an innovation you've built. One of my students is making a high-end French cuisine cooking torch for intricate meals. He's created that product and outsourced where to get it from China and have it made, and he's actually going to be releasing it on Amazon. It doesn't matter if you've got a service. What we do here is provide a service. We help people; we motivate them and help them push themselves to the next level, whether financially, with a date, or with their motivation.

Some of my students are fitness experts, and they help people with working out. Maybe you're somebody who outlines a 10-step or a 10-week method to lose lots of weight. Whatever it is, you can't make money unless you've got something specifically valuable that you can sell to make money. It could be artwork, a book, or anything you want. But you do need something to sell. There's no point in having a business where you don't have anything to sell.

If you have a 9:00 to 5:00 job right now, and you're working for somebody else, you're not actually selling anything. You are fulfilling somebody else's service, and they're selling. That's why they're your boss. They're your boss because they have something to sell and you're handling the fulfillment. You need something to sell. You could sell your own car washing services outside of work in a different area, so you don't compete with your boss. You could sell your own services coding somebody else's website. It doesn't matter what it is. If you've got a job right now, you already have a skill you could be selling. But you need to be selling it.

Next, you want to sell something that people need. There has to be a demand. There's no point being somebody who cleans cars if you live on an island like Catalina in California where no one has a car. A memorable book I read talks about how to find a crowd looking for you to sell them something. The book is called *Feed a Starving Crowd*. It's one I make every single one of my high-end clients read who want to learn about building their business or growing it. Again, maybe you've already got a business. Maybe you're already making millions of dollars. *Feed a Starving Crowd* is the key to finding more customers.

Then, build a customer base. The easiest people to sell to are the people who have already bought. I have over 50,000 followers on my YouTube channel and my email list. But the reality is we're usually selling products to the same 300 people. The same names come up over and over again, and they are the ones who will actually buy. Every so often, one of the 50,000 will add to the list, and they'll be number 301. You'll make your most money reselling to people who already bought. So, make sure whatever it is that you sell, you can resell it. If you're selling books, you want to sell a series of books, for instance.

I met an artist the other day who made beautiful artwork, but he only did one-off pieces. I told him, "You need to make a series. You need to make five pieces. That way, if somebody buys one, there's a good chance they'll buy the other four at a discount. If you're going to create one anyway, you may as well make the other four. Also, once you've sold one, you've got one person going around saying how great it is. There may be other people who want the other four."

Don't do a limited run of one, do a sequence. If you're writing books, make sure you've got part two, three, four, etc. Think about the most successful stories that you've heard of, especially in TV and the media now. *Harry Potter, Lord of the Rings*. They're multi-book series. You can even see what Marvel's doing with the Marvel Cinematic Universe. They've made a movie, and each movie leads into the next one. Think about the success of the very first Marvel movies compared to now. It's huge. That's because it's the same audience coming back. Plus, they gain more people each time with each movie. There's a reason for this. It's because it works.

If you're selling food, consider having a food subscription. A friend of mine is a chef and sells their services as a caterer to different people. I told them, "You should have a subscription. The people running events are running them on a regular basis. You might as well lock them into a subscription where they know that they're going to hire you at every single event and they don't have to worry about sourcing a different caterer each time." If you're selling a service, make sure you've got a retainer or royalties.

When I'm consulting for big marketing companies, I make them pay me a retainer every month on top of an hourly fee. So, they'll pay me $2,000 a month to be able to pick up the phone and call me to come and help them at my hourly rate. By having a regular retainer, you know that they're going to come back to you each time. The alternative to that is royalties. Meaning, every time you help them make money, you get a percentage of that fee.

Step four is the best: Make the money. You're going to find the audience to sell to. Let's just say you want to make extra money by being an Uber driver. Every single customer who gets in the car with you is a potential customer you can sell your service to.

If you're a fitness person, in your car you could have a couple of little fitness tools, like the hand exercisers, and resistance bands, whatever people can play with while they're with you. As they do, it will bring up the conversation that you're a fitness consultant, that you help people with coaching and that you drive Uber as a way of meeting new clients. You might get a new client once every other day. But the point is, you're getting paid to find customers. You've found that audience.

Another great way to find customers is to sell to businesses. Whatever it is that you're selling, do a business version of it. If you are a fitness person, rather than selling to an individual, you could contact businesses and try to sell an entire business on your plan. That way, they can get a discount because they're buying in bulk. But, more importantly, it means you can get businesses' contact details. You can pay somebody on a website like Fiverr.com to give you the contact details of every single business of a certain type in your area. It costs you $5 to get all of those contact details. A friend of mine has a business selling bows and arrows. He contacts summer camps. Again, he just pays $5 to get a list of all the summer camps in the area. One by one he contacts them. He sends them free samples: "Hey, check this out. See what you think about it." This is an easy way to make traction.

But if you're looking for an audience, don't sell to your friends. Your friends are your friends. They don't need you selling stuff to them. If they see that you're selling to other people and they're interested, they'll come to you and ask if they can work for you or if they can hire you for your services. But don't sell to friends. It's cheesy; it's not cool, and it's not the best way to get your product or service out there.

Always sell what people want at a price they can pay. Don't sell cheap. Let's say you're selling artwork; you don't want to sell it cheaply. You want to sell at a price people can afford. The easy way to do that is to find what kind of price people are already paying. So, if a friend of yours has artwork in their house, you can ask them, "How much did you pay for that?" This gives you a good idea of how to price for people who are earning the same kind of money as your friend. But you don't want to price yourself too cheap either, because then you will end up burning out, spending a lot of your time selling and you won't get that much money for it. So, make sure you're pricing at a competitive level. Instead of making your product cheaper, think about increasing the quality of the product.

Which brings us to our final point: You want to deliver an incredible product that is constantly improving. People who have been with us from the very beginning in the Facebook group notice the quality of the videos has improved every couple of months. We're always thinking of ways that we can make it better, and better, and better. In fact, over the last five weeks, there've been huge leaps and bounds in the quality of the production that we're creating. The very first time we did it though, we weren't thinking, *it has to be perfect because we're releasing it.* Otherwise, we'd have waited a year and a half to even get to where we are today. Instead, we released it and tried to deliver the best product we can. We're still constantly trying to improve it.

Sure, every so often we lose customers, and some of those customers are going to say, "This isn't the quality that I wanted." At which point we can ask them, "What changes would you have liked to see?" They will suggest the changes; we'll make the changes, and then we'll reach back out to the customer saying, "We made the changes you suggested. Would you consider coming back?" Once again, by focusing on quality and improving it rather than trying to get it perfect or trying to give a discount, you will have a much better chance of earning a decent amount of money and building a great quality product.

I'm going to leave you with a quote that has helped me get through a lot of trying times. I think it's one of the most prolific things anyone ever said to me. My dad told me, "If you enjoy what you do for work, you will never work a day in your life." I live by that. If you look back at my life and at the things I've done, the ways I've made money have almost always been doing things I enjoy. I loved the dating industry so much; I loved learning how to meet women so much that it became my job. Then I started loving my business so much and growing my business that it became my job. Previous to that, I loved doing live role-play and *Magic: The Gathering*, and so *that* became my job.

Every single thing that I love doing, I always try and think of a way to make money from it. But I don't stop doing the 9:00 to 5:00 while I'm doing it. I do it in addition. What that means is I know that I'm paying all my bills and I'm doing absolutely everything with my day job that I can. Then I take my free time, and I put that toward doing something I love to do to make money. If it starts making money, then I can transition into it when it's making enough to become my new way of making bread and butter, or I can add it onto my existing workload.

Next Steps: I hope this chapter has inspired you to take those first steps to making more money. In summary, all you have to do is look at your life and the areas where you could carve out more free time, to develop something new that you could sell to help you start to make more money. You can use the Facebook group and the following link to get involved and engage in discussions with people on their posts. You can open up discussions of your own as well. We've provided a bunch of resources to our group to help you work out what your next step should be. Check it out here: PsychologyHacker.com/Group

Chapter 12: The One Step You Need to Take to Kill Your Negative Voice

Now my question for you is, does this make sense to you? Does everything I've said here make sense? Can you feel somewhere inside you that this all just feels right?

I have another concept I discuss with my clients, something we like to call "the truth." I feel it when something makes sense when I hear it, and I'm like, "You know what? If I look back over my life, I've seen evidence of that. I've seen that this might actually be true." I want you to take a moment and think back over your life. Has what I've said here resonated with you? Do you think this might be the reason you have struggled to get what you want in life?

Maybe you've had the experience of your parents holding you back, and you can sometimes even hear them in your mind. If you've heard that voice telling you that you shouldn't do something, that's the mentor. It's just reminding you of your past experiences.

Maybe you've had the opposite experience. Maybe you've had someone teach you about a subject once, and you weren't sure you would succeed, but you had that voice in your head saying, "If you just do this, it's probably going to work." Then you did it, and it worked.

If this rings true to you, if this makes sense, I have one question for you. Do you want to kill that negative voice in your head?

Because you can kill that negative voice in your head if you follow the one step that I'm about to tell you. Now to be fair, I've actually already hinted at this one step all through this book and in the explanations of how your brain works. But here it is in plain language...

To kill the negative voice, you have to do one thing: You have to educate your mentor.

Your mentor needs to grow. You need to change the experiences it gets from negative ones to positive ones. You need to make sure that your mentor is educated in a way that leads to success so that it knows exactly what steps you have to take to achieve success and fulfillment.

Now, you can do this with your active brain, but only in situations where you're not stressed. In those times, you can sit down, and you can study, and you can learn, or you can talk to somebody who can tell you about experiences where they've had success and what steps they took to reach that success. You can then follow those steps yourself and succeed in whatever you want.

But...when you're stressed, worried, or have any fear whatsoever; you're stuck in survival mode. In those times, you need a real-life mentor who has been trained to help you make the right choices. So, you can fight back, take action, and be driven to the success you want to have.

This is where I want to help you.

I want to help you train your internal mentor in a way that can change your life.

If you get the wrong real-life mentor, you're going to get the wrong experiences. If you get a mentor talking about how great they are and how wonderful they are and how awesome they are, they're not going to help you because they're not breaking it down. The mentor in your brain needs it to be broken down.

Your mentor can't just *hear* what to do; it needs to know the psychology behind why things are happening because it has to *know* the results will be real. If the mentor doesn't believe it will work, then it's going to default to the past experiences where everything failed.

Many people make the mistake of finding somebody who's successful and thinking they're going to follow that person and learn from them. However, they don't learn anything because they only see how great the other person is. But because that person can't break down how to succeed, they can't train your internal mentor.

You need success broken down into simple steps and to understand why these steps work, because if you're going to get your mentor to communicate correctly and side with your true fan in its war with the negative voice, your mentor needs to believe. It needs to know that what you're saying is real, will work, and will get you where you want to be. This is why you need someone to break it down in detail.

You're at a crossroads, and there are a couple of ways you can proceed. You can go out and do this on your own. It's possible. You can get a whole bunch of books and read them and learn from them. You can try and calculate whether what you're reading is real or if it's marketing material. Just know that you need to recognize and avoid the people who have Googled a mix of theories they felt sounded cool and then packaged it as a book or a training program to try and get some money out of you. Unfortunately, those people do exist.

You also need to try and avoid somebody who's successful in their own life, but they don't know how they did it. They weren't ever actually a failure. I meet a lot of those guys in the business world, people who came from success and have always been great, who then try to teach you how to do it. I don't trust those people. I don't trust somebody who's always been great. It's not that their success is fake or that I resent it; I would just rather learn from someone who came from failure. I resonate with that because I wasn't always great.

If I want someone to help me, I'd like to know they've been through a rough journey and overcome it. More importantly, I'd like to know that they've helped other people. I like to see that they have taught people who've gone on to become successful. That's how I know that they're a good person to train my internal mentor. They're the people that I'll find to work with, and that I want to work with.

So yes, you can do this all on your own.

But there is another way.

You don't have to make this journey on your own. One of the primary goals of Psychology Hacker is to help people train their mentor for success. That's literally what our company does. I built Psychology Hacker for this one purpose. I want to help people understand the processes that are going on inside their brain and to help them learn how to control them.

That's one of the big things that motivates me. I get terribly sad when I hear someone say, "I don't know why this happens," or worse, "I don't know why this keeps happening to me," or even, "I can't do it and I don't know why I can't do it."

If that is you, I want to help you understand. I want you to know why things happen so even if things don't work out, at least you can say, "I understand why this decision turned out the way it did. I get why it happened, and now I know what steps to take to fix it."

The other reason I run this company is that I'm looking for me. I want to find other me's. I want to find people who are unhappy in life, who don't have the success they want, and who feel everything keeps being taken away from them or is slipping through their fingers.

I know what it's like to earn minimum wage. I know exactly what it's like to have no money and to have someone tell me, "You should save," and in my head, I'm thinking, *save what? How can I save when there's no money?*

However, I also know what it's like to be successful and to have money but to see that money invested in somebody who isn't treating me well and allowing my entire life to fall apart because I'm just supporting somebody else who doesn't care for me.

I also know what it's like to be successful and to have a lot of money and to want to push and improve but not to know which way to go. I've been there, too.

That's why I want to find the me's out there. I want to find the me who has no money, doesn't know what to do and who wants to improve, who wants to make more money, who wants to be more successful.

I want to find the me who is in that situation where they're making money, but they're giving it to somebody else and their life sucks. They're in a relationship they shouldn't be in. They're dating the wrong person. They know it, but they don't think they can do any better.

I want to find the me who's successful but wants to go to the next level, to surpass their own limits, to be even better, to make better choices, to take some risks that are actually going to pay out and make them even more successful.

I want to find those other me's and I want to help them because that's what I did. I've managed to push myself into a situation that I never thought I would see in my lifetime. At the age of 37, to have all of these experiences, to be where I am, I can only dream about what the future is going to be like.

Warren Buffett didn't start making his billions and becoming as rich as he is now until he was around 50 years old. I look at him, and I think, wow, I've got 14 more years to go to become even more successful.

That's what I'm excited about. I'm excited to push myself there, and I'm excited to help other people get there as well. So, if you're interested, if at any point you have thought, yes, I want to do this; yes, I want to improve; yes, this makes sense, you're in the right place.

Because if this is you, if this has resonated with you, I want to help.

I run a very special training program called the Internal Advancement Institute. It's where we help people train their mentors for success.

There are multiple levels within the institute, with prices that make sense for different income brackets. The programs range from the associate level, where you have access to all our classes and instructors, to those who choose to mentor under me directly.

You can't just choose to join the institute. You need to apply via our admissions team. There is a two-step interview process where we'll make sure you're a good fit for our school. We only have so many resources, and we want to be sure our focus is on helping our students get the best results they can.

We want people who are dedicated to improving their life. This is important, as it ensures all the students within the institute are of a like mind and are encouraging each other, and you, to success.

If you would like to be considered for our institute, you will find an application at the following link:

PsychologyHacker.com/Apply

It doesn't cost anything to start the application process, so you have nothing to lose.

The truth is this: Just like the experiments in the earlier chapters, the only thing it takes to apply is making the decision to overwrite that negative voice and allowing yourself to dare to let your true fan let you have the success you want.

Now I know this isn't going to be for everybody. I know some people are going to read this and say, "I think I can do this on my own." They're going to go away and not do anything, but they're going to think they will, and that's fine because we don't want to work with those people. They're not ready to change.

Many of the most successful people in the world mentored under others. Warren Buffett mentored under Benjamin Graham. Neil Strauss mentored under a guy named Eric who is better known as "Mystery" from the VH1 TV show. I mentored under that crazy Viking and a whole bunch of other people since then who have literally and completely changed my life to where it is today.

My life changed because I found the right kinds of mentors. If you want to reprogram your internal mentor, then you need to get the right kind of real-life mentors in your life, too.

We've built the Internal Advancement Institute to help people. We want to help people who don't make a lot of money improve their life, and to help people who do make a lot of money but want to take their success to that next level.

If you do want to come work with us, I'm excited, and I want to work with you. I would love to work directly with all of you, but I only have so many hours in a day. I do want to spend time with my family, and I want to keep pushing myself to succeed in my own journey. Most of my growth comes from working on my life and finding out what I want to change and improve. However, I still love working with people. I love finding other me's.

If you've got the right kind of attitude, if you really want to succeed, if you're going to push yourself hard, there's something for you in our institute. There's no one there who doesn't want to work to push themselves hard. If you're willing to invest the time and money, it's going to take to succeed; then you should take the chance to apply.

I created the institute with one purpose: to put together a group of people who are dedicated to improving. They don't argue with each other. They don't throw insults around. You get kicked out of the institute straightaway if you do any of those kinds of things. The students within the institute just want to succeed.

The institute is literally living evidence that this stuff works. There are people in there who have turned around their life financially. There are people who have turned around their relationship life. They've managed to finally get rid of that dry spell where they weren't dating for a long time, and now they're having a lot of meaningful, loving relationships.

The Internal Advancement Institute is probably the best thing I've created in my entire business life. I love the institute. Go to this link, fill in the form, and find out what it's all about:

PsychologyHacker.com/Apply

Again, we can't guarantee you will get in. We're going to pick and choose the people we think are going to put in the right effort and are going to stick with it, the people who won't stay for a month and think, *oh, that was fun. I got a whole bunch of cool stuff, and now I'm gone.*

When you first sign up, you get access to lots of training seminars on how to be more attractive, how to take action and get the things you want, and even more information on how to defeat that negative voice.

You get all these seminars as a bonus, and then you can access the institute itself, where you can attend even more regular classes that take place every single week.

Plus, you get access to a private online group where you can communicate with the other students and, more importantly, ask questions and have experts like my team and me participate in the discussion and answer them.

The three different levels of the Internal Advancement Institute are very simple. We have the regular membership level, where the initial signup is $297 for the first month, and it's only $197 a month to continue after that. Most people stay in it for life because they're constantly improving. It doesn't take long before you can start focusing on the financial aspect of your life and make more than enough money to cover the membership and more.

Then, of course, there are all the other benefits you get from building up your social or dating life. You'll meet great friends to work with you, and you can brainstorm on whatever financial or personal project you want to work on.

At the next level, which we call the Experience, members have access to all of the above but also gain access to our Experience events, where they meet and work with our team in person twice a year. At the Experience, we hand-guide people through taking the actual action steps necessary to build and achieve the success they want.

Imagine having someone walk you through every step of starting a business piece by piece. Or taking you out to a venue and teaching you how to network in person.

That's just for starters. The Experience goes well beyond that. We teach many of the students additional life skills, like traveling around the world for less than $700 and more.

The highest level at the institute is mentoring under me. You'll get access to my personal cell phone. You can talk to me, and I will guide you through the exact steps not just that I took but the exact steps that all of the literally hundreds of people I've trained have taken who have gone on to enjoy success in every area of their life, from love to income and so much more.

One of my students contacted me the other day and told me he now raises large sums of capital for tech firms around the world.

I have other students who have gone from working retail to becoming very powerful lawyers.

I've had people who've gone from having only a video camera to making literally some of the best and biggest videos on YouTube, with millions and millions of views.

In short, I've helped a lot of different people succeed in a lot of different areas. For those of you who pass through the application process and get to work with me, I'm going to share with you what I've learned on my own and what my mentors taught me to build and enjoy the life I currently have.

Here's what I want you to do. If you think yes, you want to do this, you want to improve, then do me a favor. More importantly, do yourself a favor:

Go to the site below and fill in the application form. It costs nothing, to start the process.

PsychologyHacker.com/Apply

After you fill in the form, your application will go through to my department, where we'll interview you to find out if you're right for the Internal Advancement Institute.

As I said, it is an institution. We don't let just anybody in. We have to vet you, to make sure you have the right mental attitude, that you're going to stick with it and that you're going to succeed. We need to know you're the type of person who's going to put in the effort. Because we're going to put a lot of time and effort into helping you improve. I want to make sure you're actually doing what you've been taught.

So, fill in the application form. Make sure you put your best foot forward. I promise you, if you take that step right now, if you take that step to action and you keep it going, then we can kill that negative voice within you. We can make it go away. We can make your internal mentor stronger and give that voice actual experience in what to do and how to succeed in all sorts of situations. Then your true fan will be the voice that supports you.

In that way, whether you're actively trying to control your life, or you're just passively coasting through and letting your true fan and the mentor give you all the success you want, you can simply relax, enjoy it, and see as, year after year, your life gets better and better and better.

Here's that form one last time...

PsychologyHacker.com/Apply

Chapter 13: Conclusion

There are a few things I'm really proud of when it comes to my own work. The content in this book is one of them. I've sat at business meetings with multimillionaires and shared the content within these pages and had people fighting over each other to work with me.

These are successful people who realized that if they could kill that voice of self-doubt in their mind, they could achieve so much more.

As humans we like to think we're smart; we like to think things are complicated. But the reality is we're operating with the same hardware that we have used for 150,000 years.

The technology has changed, but we're as naturally smart as the cave dwellers we used to be.

Remember, your brain has one primary focus, and that's to keep you alive. It would prefer you to be happy, but that comes second.

Your subconscious is mostly operating on autopilot to conserve energy for life-threatening situations that may or may not happen.

Whenever you're stressed or worried, you're trapped in that state.

The only way you can get out of it is to train your subconscious for success.

You do that by training your internal mentor and teaching it what it needs to do.

You do it by hacking your brain for success.

Soon it becomes so automatic, you barely even notice how easy it is to get everything you've ever wanted.

Afterword

Thanks so much for reading this book. The truth is, I sat pumping it out in a 48-hour time span in a Starbucks in a frantic writing session after a burst of inspiration and a desire to get this information into as many hands as possible.

A week earlier, I was giving a talk to someone running for Congress, and I shared the information in this book with him. Soon, other people in the room gravitated to my talk, and suddenly I was training 12 CEOs on how their brain operated.

It made me realize I hadn't worked hard enough to get this information out there. It got me focused and desperate to find a way to get it out quickly to help as many people as possible.

The content in these pages saved my life in many ways. If we ever meet in person, I'll be happy to tell you exactly what I mean.

In the meantime, I hope this inspires you to think about how you make decisions.

I hope it helps you understand the things you feel are unexplainable. But above all, I hope it changes your life the way it changed mine.

References

1. Kahneman, Daniel. *Thinking, Fast and Slow*. New York: Farrar, Straus and Giroux, 2015.

2. Coorey, Robert. *Feed a Starving Crowd: More Than 200 Hot and Fresh Marketing Strategies to Help You Find Hungry Customers.* Lake Placid, NY: Aviva Publishing, 2014.

About the Author

Adam Lyons is the CEO of Psychology Hacker and Tao of Badass. He is the Founder of the Internal Advancement Institute, and Director at Social Training Company. His accomplishments in his personal and business life have earned him Columnist positions at FHM and Askmen.com, and the 2 Comma-Club Award (ClickFunnels). In addition, he is an author, innovator, and mindset master dedicated to helping people develop their own abilities to continually self-improve.

Adam grew up in a poor family in one of the rougher areas of London. There weren't a lot of luxuries and even fights over food at dinnertime.

Today, he lives on a 40-acre ranch just outside of Austin, Texas. He owns two houses, drives a Maserati, and has founded several successful companies that made him over a million dollars in the past year. Most importantly, his family has NEVER had to argue over who was getting the last scrap of food.

So... how did he get from point A to point B?

The simple answer is: Persistence.

Adam has always had a natural passion for psychology and human interaction. He *loves* studying how people think, which naturally led him to the first step of his career: public relations.

Although he started off as a janitor in one of the biggest PR firms in London, it wasn't long before he'd impressed the staff enough to begin doing analytical work. Over the years, he learned the ins and outs of some of the biggest businesses in London and seeing how they worked with the community to ensure a positive public image. Whether it was a small mom-and-pop grocery store or a massive car company like Bentley, they all used the same basic system to keep themselves in check.

After studying their methodologies enough, all the puzzle pieces began to fall in place, and he came upon a revelation.

If companies could follow these strategies to make sure the public loved them...why couldn't people do that, too?

With this idea in mind, he founded The Social Training Company, a group dedicated to applying the same techniques used by multimillion dollar companies to personal interaction.

Whether it's a shy office worker trying to ask for a raise from his boss or two broke college kids who have a billion-dollar idea for the next tech startup, Adam wanted to give them the tools they'd need to get the job done. The same tools that he'd spent years developing on his own.

The results speak for themselves. After the initial success of The Social Training Company, Adam discovered that the market was ripe with people looking for answers in all aspects of their personal life. This led him to branch out, and he built several brands from the ground-up to offer tailor-made solutions for everything from personal confidence to financial management.

Even more importantly, he's developed a community of people who have used his services over the years. In fact, many of them have worked for him at one point or another, which ensures that his companies will continue to grow and improve.

Of course, ever the entrepreneur, Adam is always looking for new opportunities to reach out to new people. So, when the opportunity arose to work with Tucker Max on a book designed to provide these ideas to readers everywhere, he jumped at the chance. Through the ideas in this book and the myriad of other programs that he offers, Adam is hoping to provide readers with all of the same skills and techniques he used to go from being a janitor to becoming a millionaire.

Made in the USA
Middletown, DE
31 August 2018